CONTEMPORARY ISSUES COMPANION

Marijuana

Other Books of Related Interest:

Marijuana

Joseph Tardiff, Book Editor

GREENHAVEN PRESS

An imprint of Thomson Gale, a part of The Thomson Corporation

THOMSON
━━━━━━★━━━━━━
GALE

Detroit • New York • San Francisco • New Haven, Conn. • Waterville, Maine • London

Christine Nasso, *Publisher*
Elizabeth Des Chenes, *Managing Editor*

© 2008 The Gale Group.

Star logo is a trademark and Gale and Greenhaven Press are registered trademarks used herein under license.

For more information, contact:
Greenhaven Press
27500 Drake Rd.
Farmington Hills, MI 48331-3535
Or you can visit our Internet site at http://www.gale.com

LIBRARY OF CONGRESS CATALOGING-IN-PUBLICATION DATA

Marijuana / Joe Tardiff, book editor.
    p. cm. -- (Contemporary issues companion)
  Includes bibliographical references and index.
  ISBN-13: 978-0-7377-2775-3 (hardcover)
  ISBN-13: 978-0-7377-2776-0 (pbk.)
  1. Marijuana abuse--United States. 2. Marijuana--Physiological effect.
3. Marijuana--Therapeutic use. 4. Drug legalization--United States. 5.
Drug control--United States. I. Tardiff, Joseph C., 1966-
  HV5825.M353 2008
  362.29'50973--dc22
                                                                2007026489

ISBN-10: 0-7377-2775-6 (hardcover)
ISBN-10: 0-7377-2776-4 (pbk.)

Printed in the United States of America
10 9 8 7 6 5 4 3 2 1

Contents

Foreword

In the news, on the streets, and in neighborhoods, individuals are confronted with a variety of social problems. Such problems may affect people directly: A young woman may struggle with depression, suspect a friend of having bulimia, or watch a loved one battle cancer. And even the issues that do not directly affect her private life—such as religious cults, domestic violence, or legalized gambling—still impact the larger society in which she lives. Discovering and analyzing the complexities of issues that encompass communal and societal realms as well as the world of personal experience is a valuable educational goal in the modern world.

Effectively addressing social problems requires familiarity with a constantly changing stream of data. Becoming well informed about today's controversies is an intricate process that often involves reading myriad primary and secondary sources, analyzing political debates, weighing various experts' opinions—even listening to firsthand accounts of those directly affected by the issue. For students and general observers, this can be a daunting task because of the sheer volume of information available in books, periodicals, on the evening news, and on the Internet. Researching the consequences of legalized gambling, for example, might entail sifting through congressional testimony on gambling's societal effects, examining private studies on Indian gaming, perusing numerous Web sites devoted to Internet betting, and reading essays written by lottery winners as well as interviews with recovering compulsive gamblers. Obtaining valuable information can be time-consuming—since it often requires researchers to pore over numerous documents and commentaries before discovering a source relevant to their particular investigation.

Greenhaven's Contemporary Issues Companion series seeks to assist this process of research by providing readers with useful and pertinent information about today's complex issues. Each volume in this anthology series focuses on a topic of current interest, presenting informative and thought-provoking selections written from a wide variety of viewpoints. The readings selected by the editors include such diverse sources as personal accounts and case studies, pertinent factual and statistical articles, and relevant commentaries and overviews. This diversity of sources and views, found in every Contemporary Issues Companion, offers readers a broad perspective in one convenient volume.

In addition, each title in the Contemporary Issues Companion series is designed especially for young adults. The selections included in every volume are chosen for their accessibility and are expertly edited in consideration of both the reading and comprehension levels of the audience. The structure of the anthologies also enhances accessibility. An introductory essay places each issue in context and provides helpful facts such as historical background or current statistics and legislation that pertain to the topic. The chapters that follow organize the material and focus on specific aspects of the book's topic. Every essay is introduced by a brief summary of its main points and biographical information about the author. These summaries aid in comprehension and can also serve to direct readers to material of immediate interest and need. Finally, a comprehensive index allows readers to efficiently scan and locate content.

The Contemporary Issues Companion series is an ideal launching point for research on a particular topic. Each anthology in the series is composed of readings taken from an extensive gamut of resources, including periodicals, newspapers, books, government documents, the publications of private and public organizations, and Internet websites. In these volumes, readers will find factual support suitable for use in reports, debates, speeches, and research papers. The anthologies also facilitate further research, featuring a book and periodical bibliography and a list of organizations to contact for additional information.

A perfect resource for both students and the general reader, Greenhaven's Contemporary Issues Companion series is sure to be a valued source of current, readable information on social problems that interest young adults. It is the editors' hope that readers will find the Contemporary Issues Companion series useful as a starting point to formulate their own opinions about and answers to the complex issues of the present day.

Introduction

Marijuana use is one of the most polarizing social issues in the United States today. While viewpoints on the subject are remarkably diverse—indeed often strident—in their opposition to one another, there is one point on which most parties agree: Marijuana should be kept away from kids. Sponsored by the National Institute on Drug Abuse (NIDA), the Monitoring the Future survey has tracked adolescent illicit drug use since 1975. According to the survey's 2006 findings, marijuana is by far the most widely used illicit drug by teenagers. The survey shows that some 12 percent of eighth graders, 25 percent of tenth graders, and 32 percent of twelfth graders have at least experimented with marijuana. Further, a 2005 Monitoring the Future report indicates that 41 percent of eighth graders, 73 percent of tenth graders, and 86 percent of twelfth graders have stated that marijuana is highly accessible.

Through the combined efforts of the White House Office of National Drug Control Policy (ONDCP), the U.S. Drug Enforcement Administration (DEA), and state and local law enforcement agencies, the federal government has waged a massive war on drugs since the early 1980s, emphasizing the prohibition of marijuana as a cornerstone of their strategy. A major component of this initiative involves the government funding of public service announcements and educational programs designed to warn adolescents about the dangers of getting involved with drugs. The government also supports student drug testing as a means to prevent and treat adolescent drug use, maintaining that the practice increases parental and community awareness, helps teens resist peer pressure, and reduces potential drug dependence. Further, a number of government agencies have conducted or sponsored scientific studies to evaluate the harmful short- and long-term health effects of smoking marijuana, the potentially dangerous consequences of driving while under the influence of pot, and marijuana's role as a gateway drug.

The gateway drug debate has become perhaps one of the most controversial aspects of the government's antidrug position. The government has been steadfast in its assertion that far from being an innocuous recreational drug, marijuana in fact can induce users—especially impressionable adolescent users—into experimenting with even more harmful and addictive drugs. According to the ONDCP, studies have shown that early marijuana users are eight times as likely to use cocaine, fifteen times as likely to use heroin, and five times as likely to develop some kind of dependence on any drug.[1] Detractors have countered that government-endorsed studies identifying marijuana as a gateway drug are inconclusive at best and that any number of factors—including biological, psychological, and environmental influences—could be responsible for persuading people to try hard drugs. Ethan A. Nadelmann, the director of the Drug Policy Alliance, maintains that if "marijuana did not exist, there's little reason to believe that there would be less drug abuse in the U.S.; indeed, its role would most likely be filled by a more dangerous substance."[2]

The federal government also has aggressively pursued drug law enforcement through the arrest, prosecution, and incarceration of marijuana users, cultivators, and distributors. Because of their age, minors generally have avoided the harsh legal penalties associated with getting arrested for marijuana possession. But critics of the government's policy of zero tolerance for drug law offenders contend that the system arrests and jails a disproportionate number of adult offenders for mere possession of marijuana rather than going after major traffickers who are responsible for the drug's wide-scale distribution. In fact, a 2005 study conducted by the Sentencing Project—an advocacy group which promotes the reform of traditional approaches to sentencing and incarcerating criminals—reveals that 90 percent of marijuana arrests in 2002 were for possession, not drug dealing or trafficking; further, those convicted of possession served an average of sixteen months in prison, while convicted traffickers received prison terms averaging only nine months.

Some critics of zero-tolerance laws have speculated that incarceration associated with minor drug offenses could ultimately have the unintended consequence of creating a broken family environment which, in turn, might cause a child to engage in delinquent behavior, including drug use. Mikki Norris, the founder and director of the Cannabis Consumer Campaign, recounts the story of Jodie Israel: "She was a young mother who was sentenced to 11 years as a first-time, non-violent marijuana user along with her husband who was sentenced to 29 years. The government orphaned their four children, and they were forced to live in four different homes when their parents went to prison."[3]

Whereas the federal government has implemented an unambiguous and aggressive program to prohibit drug use in America, many parents face an ethical dilemma when it comes to addressing marijuana use with their children. Indeed, "baby boomer" parents who experimented with pot and other drugs during the 1960s, as well as subsequent generations of marijuana users, have had to devise strategies to explain the harmful consequences of marijuana use without appearing hypocritical to their children. Further, parents who continue to smoke pot recreationally find themselves in an even more precarious position when it comes to talking about drug use with their kids. Observing that most of these parents have "turned into impressive and able members of the republic," Larry Smith goes on to write that "these are people with good jobs, who engage in charitable pursuits and who rarely cut in the line at Whole Foods. We've taken some of our old vices with us into adulthood without burning down the house or checking into rehab. We've done a good job prolonging our adolescence, but now we're facing adulthood's ultimate gut check: children."[4]

Whether parents are past or present marijuana users, they face tough choices when it comes to talking about drugs with their children. Some elect to be completely honest with their kids about their own past, explaining what they perceive to be the benefits and pitfalls of smoking pot based on their own experiences with the drug. Others have taken a need-to-know approach to communicating with their children, discussing the potential consequences of smoking marijuana without revealing the more unseemly aspects of their own personal drug experiences. Still other parents elect to conceal their past and present experiences with marijuana and tell their kids that getting involved with drugs is just plain wrong. Most parents would agree, however, that open and honest communication about the potential risks and rewards involved in smoking marijuana is the most productive approach to educating their children.

A 2002 study underscores the significance of parental influence on the choices that kids make. The survey of youths whose ages ranged from twelve to seventeen showed that nearly 90 percent of the respondents believed that their parents would strongly disapprove of them trying marijuana once or twice. The survey also demonstrated that recent marijuana use was lower among children who believed that parents would disapprove of their actions; indeed, 27 percent of youths who felt that their parents would not disapprove of their actions reported past-month use of marijuana, whereas only 4.9 percent of kids who felt that their parents would disapprove indicated that they used the drug in the prior month.[5] The ONDCP states, "people are surprised to learn that parents are the most powerful influence on their children when it comes to drugs. By staying involved, knowing what their kids are doing, and setting limits with clear rules and consequences, parents can increase the chances their kids will stay drug free."[6]

Reformers who would like to see marijuana legalized and regulated like alcohol and tobacco offer another perspective on keeping pot away from children. This group asserts that the government should legalize marijuana and then levy a sales tax of as much as 1,000 percent on the drug. As a result, the cost for purchasing marijuana would be prohibitive to minors and therefore deter them from using it. Daniel Sumner, an agricultural economist at the University of California, argues "that it makes more sense to tax things than to ban them. You generate revenue and you give people an incentive to behave the way we want."[7]

However, reformers acknowledge that regulating marijuana probably will not deter all minors from experimenting with the drug. Indeed, they recognize that many kids will still succumb to the allure of trying something that is forbidden, especially if it becomes more accessible through decriminalization. Despite this observation, reformers point to a U.S. Department of Health and Human Services survey which demonstrates that some 15 percent of eighth graders, 33 percent of tenth graders, and 37 percent of twelfth graders experimented with pot in 2001. That same survey shows that 12 percent of eighth graders, 21 percent of tenth graders, and 30 percent of twelfth graders also smoked cigarettes, statistics that are nearly identical to marijuana use. Based on these results, some reform advocates speculate that adolescents might smoke even less marijuana if its mystique is removed by legalization.

Critics of this proposed policy point out that while alcohol and tobacco are legal and regulated for adult consumption, nevertheless both drugs still pose significant risks for minors who are able to obtain them through illicit means. Decriminalizing marijuana and adding it to the mix of potentially threatening legal drugs that are readily available, these detractors contend, will only increase the overall challenge of preventing underage consumers from using and abusing drugs. Still other critics argue that aside from the potentially harmful consequences of increased accessibility to marijuana, teenagers who smoke pot are more likely to become sedentary and antisocial. Steve Sailer remarks that smoking dope "may not do all that many of the horrible things often attributed to it, but it definitely makes people want to sit down. And that's something that even the most clean and sober young people of the 21st Century do way too much of already."[8]

Despite universal concern about children and marijuana use, the fact remains that popular culture as a whole provides an ambivalent, perhaps even positive, perception of pot. Kids often see marijuana use depicted in the popular media as a normal, socially acceptable recreational activity. They view tabloid reports of their favorite celebrities and athletes who use and abuse marijuana but who do not suffer any overly punitive consequences for committing drug crimes. While the pop culture glamorizes marijuana, it also minimizes the drug's potential harmful effects, including long-term health problems, addiction, and jail time. Authority figures, whether they are parents, the government, or drug law reformers and policy makers, all face significant obstacles when it comes to challenging marijuana's overwhelmingly positive image in our popular culture. Persistent education and communication are perhaps the most crucial tools in shaping the minds and actions of America's kids.

Notes

1. Office of National Drug Control Policy, *What Americans Need to Know About Marijuana: Important Facts About Our Nation's Most Misunderstood Illicit Drug.* Rockville, MD: Office of National Drug Control Policy, October 2003.
2. Ethan A. Nadelmann, "An End to Marijuana Prohibition," *National Review*, July 12, 2004, p. 30.
3. Quoted in Simone Mariotti, "Cannabis: Why Prohibition Is Harmful—An Interview with Mikki Norris," *La Voce di Romagna*, August 11, 2005 (available on the Cannabis Consumers Campaign Web site, http://cannabisconsumers.org/art_view.php?rec_num=78).

4. Larry Smith, "Do You Puff, Daddy?" *Salon*, July 13, 2004, http://dir.salon.com/story/mwt/feature/2004/07/13/drugs/index.html.

5. Substance Abuse and Mental Health Services Administration, *2002 National Household Survey on Drug Abuse Report: Parental Disapproval of Youths' Substance Abuse*. Rockville, MD: Substance Abuse and Mental Health Services Administration, 2002. This report is based on data from the *2000 National Household Survey on Drug Abuse Report*.

6. Office of National Drug Control Policy, *Marijuana Myths and Facts: The Truth Behind 10 Popular Misperceptions*. Rockville, MD: Office of National Drug Control Policy, November 2001, p. 19.

7. Quoted in David Lazarus, "State's Untapped Pot of Gold," *San Francisco Chronicle*, March 1, 2002, www.sfgate.com/cgi-bin/article.cgi?file=/chronicle/archive/2002/03/01/BU170466.DTL&type=business.

8. Steve Sailer, "The Kids Are Alwrong," *American Spectator*, September 7, 2004, www.spectator.org/dsp_article.asp?art_id=7043.

CHAPTER 1

The Impact of Marijuana Use

Marijuana Is a Bigger Problem than People Realize

Office of National Drug Control Policy

The U.S. federal government leads the effort to enforce drug laws and to prevent the use and abuse of illegal drugs, including marijuana. The White House Office of National Drug Control Policy (ONDCP)—a component of the Executive Office of the President—has prepared a report that addresses many of the commonly held notions on the use and misuse of marijuana in the United States. The report dispels a number of popular myths and misconceptions relating to marijuana use and discusses the federal government's mission to restrict access to the drug. Further, the paper calls for civic involvement in dealing with the marijuana problem and advocates a number of substance-abuse treatment programs for addicts. The study concludes with a brief survey of issues related to marijuana use, including the legalization movement, medical marijuana, and drug testing in schools.

There is a serious drug problem in this country, and marijuana is a much bigger part of the problem than most people realize.

- Marijuana is the most widely used illicit drug in America. Of the nearly 20 million current illicit drug users, 14.6 million (about 75 percent) are using marijuana.

- Of the 7.1 million Americans suffering from illegal drug dependence or abuse, 60 percent abuse or are dependent on marijuana.

Office of National Drug Control Policy, "What Americans Need to Know About Marijuana: Important Facts About Our Nation's Most Misunderstood Illegal Drug," October 2003, pp. 1–11.

- More young people are now in treatment for marijuana dependency than for alcohol or for all other illegal drugs combined.

- Of all youth age 12–17 in drug treatment in 2000, nearly 62 percent had a primary marijuana diagnosis. Approximately half were referred to treatment through the criminal justice system and half through other sources, including self-referral.

- The average age of initiation for marijuana use generally has been getting younger.

Along with the bad news, however, come signs of improvement:

- Among 10th graders, past-year and past-month use of marijuana or hashish decreased from 2001 to 2002, as did daily use in the past month.

- There has been slow but steady progress toward reduced marijuana use rates among 8th graders. Their past-year marijuana-use rate of 14.6 percent in 2002 is the lowest since 1994, and well below their recent peak of 18.3 percent in 1996.

- At 30.3 percent for past-year marijuana use, 10th graders are at their lowest level since 1995 and somewhat below their recent peak of 34.8 percent in 1997. The past-year use rate for 12th graders is down, albeit only modestly, from 38.5 percent in their recent peak year (1997) to 36.2 percent in 2002.

Myth One: *Marijuana Is Harmless*

Marijuana is far from harmless; in fact, recent scientific findings about the drug are startling. Most of the drug treatment for young people in the United States is for marijuana alone. Marijuana emergency-room mentions have skyrocketed over the past decade, and the drug is associated with an increased risk of developing schizophrenia, even when personality traits and pre-existing conditions are taken into account.

FACTS:

Health Consequences:

- Marijuana smoke contains 50 percent to 70 percent more carcinogenic hydrocarbons than does tobacco smoke. Using marijuana may promote cancer of the respiratory tract and disrupt the immune system.

- Marijuana smokers have a heightened risk of lung infection.

- Long-term use of marijuana may increase the risk of chronic cough, bronchitis, and emphysema, as well as cancer of the head, neck, and lungs.

- Mentions of marijuana use in emergency room visits have risen 176 percent since 1994, surpassing those of heroin.

- In 2001, marijuana was a contributing factor in more than 110,000 emergency department visits in the United States.

- Smoking marijuana leads to changes in the brain similar to those caused by the use of cocaine and heroin.

- Marijuana can cause the heart rate, normally 70 to 80 beats per minute, to increase by 20 to 50 beats per minute or, in some cases, even to double.

- In a 2003 study, researchers in England found that smoking marijuana for even less than six years causes a marked deterioriation in lung function. The study suggests that marijuana use may rob the body of antioxidants that protect cells against damage that can lead to heart disease and cancer.

- The British Lung Foundation reports that smoking three or four marijuana joints is as bad for your lungs as smoking 20 tobacco cigarettes.

- Marijuana affects alertness, concentration, perception, coordination, and reaction time—skills that are necessary for safe driving. A roadside study of reckless drivers in Tennessee found that 33 percent of all subjects who were not under the influence of alcohol and who were tested for drugs at the scene of their arrest tested positive for marijuana. In a 2003 Canadian study, one in five students admitted to driving within an hour of using marijuana.

- Marijuana users have more suicidal thoughts and are four times more likely to report symptoms of depression than people who never used the drug.

- The *British Medical Journal* recently reported: "Cannabis use is associated with an increased risk of developing schizophrenia, consistent with a causal relation. This association is not explained by use of other psychoactive drugs or personality traits relating to social integration."

Social Consequences:

- Heavy marijuana use impairs the ability of young people to concentrate and retain information during their peak learning years. Tetrahydrocannabinol (THC), the main active chemical in marijuana, changes the way sensory information gets into and is processed by the part of the brain that is crucial for learning and memory.

- Animal studies indicate that marijuana use may interfere with brain function and create problems with the perception of time, possibly making the user less adept at tasks that require sustained attention.

- Marijuana use has been associated with poor performance in school. One report showed that youths with an average grade of D or below were more than four times as likely to have used marijuana in the past year as youths with an average grade of A.

- Marijuana users in their later teen years are more likely to have an increased risk of delinquency and more friends who exhibit deviant behavior. They also tend to have more sexual partners and are more likely to engage in unsafe sex.

Economic Consequences:

- Use of marijuana and other illicit drugs comes at significant expense to society in terms of lost employee productivity, public health care costs, and accidents.

- Americans spent $10.6 billion on marijuana purchases in 1999.

Myth Two: *Marijuana Is Not Addictive*

Marijuana has been proven to be a psychologically addictive drug. Scientists at the National Institute on Drug Abuse have demonstrated that laboratory animals will self-administer THC in doses equivalent to those used by humans who smoke marijuana.

FACTS:

- Marijuana is much more powerful today than it was 30 years ago, and so are its mind-altering effects. Average THC levels rose from less than 1 percent in the mid-1970s to more than 6 percent in 2002. Sinsemilla potency increased in the past two decades from 6 percent to more than 13 percent, with some samples containing THC levels of up to 33 percent.

- Subjects in an experiment on marijuana withdrawal experienced symptoms such as restlessness, loss of appetite, trouble with sleeping, weight loss, and shaky hands.

- Some heavy users of marijuana show signs of dependence, developing withdrawal symptoms when they have not used the drug for a period of time.

- According to one study, marijuana use by teenagers with prior serious antisocial problems can quickly lead to dependence on the drug. The study also found that, for troubled teenagers using tobacco, alcohol, and marijuana, progression from their first use of marijuana to regular use was about as rapid as their progression to regular tobacco use, and more rapid than the progression to regular use of alcohol.

Myth Three: *Youth Experimentation with Marijuana Is Inevitable*

Drug use can be prevented. The majority of young people do not use drugs, and there are proven ways to keep kids from starting. Contrary to popular belief, marijuana use is not a rite of passage. It is a risky behavior with serious consequences. Every American has a role to play in the effort to reduce marijuana use—at home and on the job, in schools, places of worship, and civic or social organizations. Working together, we can reaffirm healthy attitudes about marijuana use.

FACTS:

- Surveys show that parents are the biggest influence in their children's decisions about drug use. Parents must actively engage in educating their children and help them make healthy decisions.

- We know that when we push back against the drug problem, it recedes. Marijuana use has been dramatically lower in the past—even in the last decade—and it can be reduced again.

Myth Four: *Marijuana Is Not Associated with Violence*

It's not simply the trafficking of drugs that causes crime at home and abroad. Crime also results from the behavior of people who have drug dependencies.

FACTS:

- Research shows a link between frequent marijuana use and increased violent behavior.

- Young people who use marijuana weekly are nearly four times more likely than nonusers to engage in violence.

- More than 41 percent of male arrestees in sampled U.S. cities tested positive for marijuana.

Myth Five: *Prisons Are Filled with Non-Violent, Casual Marijuana Users*

Most law enforcement officials would attest that simple marijuana users rarely get sent to jail. In fact, a substantial number of states and localities rate simple possession of marijuana as a misdemeanor, subject only to a small fine. Our prisons are not filled with people whose only crime was smoking marijuana. The vast majority of those behind bars for marijuana offenses are mid- and large-scale traffickers and distributors.

FACTS:

- Less than one percent of all state prison inmates in 1997 were serving time just for marijuana possession

(0.7 percent), and only 0.3 percent of marijuana-possession offenders were in prison on a first offense.

- On the federal level, nearly 98 percent of the 7,991 offenders sentenced for marijuana crimes in 2001 were guilty of trafficking. Only 2.3 percent—186 people—were sentenced for simple possession of marijuana.

- The median amount of marijuana involved in the conviction in federal court of marijuana-only possession offenders in 1997 was 115 pounds. In other words, half of all federal prisoners convicted just for marijuana possession were arrested with quantities exceeding 115 pounds.

The Mission

Responsible public policy seeks to reduce access to and availability of marijuana. Once people know the facts about the drug, it is important that they work to develop a comprehensive approach for preventing and reducing its use. Moreover, law enforcement agencies at all levels should make it a top priority to intensify detection and removal of marijuana-growing operations.

- Curbing access to marijuana is a major challenge. A 2001 survey found that 55 percent of kids age 12–17 agreed that marijuana would be "fairly easy" or "very easy" to obtain and was available from a wide variety of sources.

Our responsibility as employers, colleagues, neighbors, family members, and friends is to get the marijuana user beyond denial and into effective treatment and lifelong recovery.

- Reduce the denial gap

- Of the 5.6 million people who met the criteria for drug dependence and abuse specified in the 4th edition of the *Diagnostic and Statistical Manual of Mental Disor-*

ders in 2001, 4.6 million (92 percent) did not acknowledge they had a problem.

- Treatment works.

- Federal spending for substance-abuse treatment has risen sharply in recent years, increasing from about $2.2 billion in 1993 to nearly $3.3 billion in 2003.

- The federal government sponsored the Cannabis Youth Treatment Study (CYT), which developed innovative and effective treatment methodologies.

- Using these treatment approaches, the percentage of young people reporting abstinence from marijuana use went from 4 percent upon entering the study to 13 percent within 3 months, and to 34 percent after 6 months. The percentage of those having no past-month symptoms of marijuana abuse or dependence went from an initial 19 percent to 39 percent within 3 months, and to 61 percent after 6 months.

- The CYT study found that brief interventions, or structured efforts to interrupt and stop an individual's drug use, could be very successful, especially with low-severity clients (such as those who are not yet dependent).

- The advantage of brief interventions is that they can be carried out in non-medical environments by non-medical staff. The screening and brief intervention approach is currently being used in a variety of settings (such as emergency rooms and social service agencies), and it has been found to be both clinically and cost effective.

- Drug courts, or supervised programs that offer alternatives to incarceration, are a common means of providing treatment for drug users. Established to handle the growing caseload of low-level drug offenses, drug courts separate non-violent users from people charged with trafficking and other serious drug crimes.

- Recidivism rates among all drug court participants have ranged from 5 percent to 28 percent; for graduates of drug courts, the recidivism rate is less than 4 percent.

- Drug courts are expanding rapidly, and the federal government is helping to fuel this growth. The President's proposed FY [Fiscal Year] 2004 budget includes an increase in drug-court funding from the currently enacted $45 million to $68 million. More than 1,000 drug courts are in operation around the country, and approximately 400 are in development. To date, some 300,000 adults and juveniles have enrolled in drug court programs.

- Communities can take action now. We urge treatment programs and providers to employ these proven methods. . . .

Related Issues

1. Marijuana v. tobacco and alcohol: the case against legalization

- Alcohol and tobacco pose significant risks, especially to young people.

- Alcohol and tobacco cost society a great deal every year in terms of crime, lost productivity, tragedies, and deaths. Why legalize marijuana and add a third drug to the current list of licit threats?

- As a result of legal settlements and vigorous public education efforts, many Americans are aware of the dangers of dependence and addiction associated with alcohol and tobacco use. Even so, alcohol and tobacco remain a significant part of the American health problem.

2. Gateway theory

- A direct cause-and-effect relationship between marijuana use and subsequent use of other drugs is hard to prove. Studies show, however, that of the people who have ever used marijuana, those who started early are more likely to have other problems later on. For example, adults who were early marijuana users were found to be:

- 8 times more likely to have used cocaine.

- 15 times more likely to have used heroin.

- 5 times more likely to develop a need for treatment of abuse or dependence on *any* drug.

- The *Journal of the American Medical Association* reported a study of more than 300 sets of same-sex twins. The study found that marijuana-using twins were four times more likely than their siblings to use cocaine and crack cocaine, and five times more likely to use hallucinogens such as LSD.

3. Medical marijuana

- Our medical system relies on proven scientific research, not polling results.

- About 100 years ago, leaders in this country created the U.S. Food and Drug Administration (FDA) to make sure that medicine falls under the "safe and effective" standard before it is sold on the open market.

- Research has not demonstrated that smoked marijuana is helpful as medicine.

- A component in marijuana—THC—has been approved in pill form by the FDA. It's called Marinol, and though it is not frequently prescribed, the U.S. supports the right of doctors to prescribe this drug if they feel it would best serve their patients' needs. The U.S. Drug Enforcement Administration (DEA) even lowered the scheduling on Marinol to make it easier for doctors to prescribe the drug.

- Marijuana smoke contains more than 400 chemicals and increases the risk of cancer, lung damage, and poor pregnancy outcomes.

- The U.S. continues to support research into the medical efficacy of certain isolated properties of marijuana.

- Even if smoking marijuana makes people "feel better," that is not enough to call it a medicine. If that were the case, tobacco cigarettes could be called medicine because they are often said to make people feel better. For that matter, heroin certainly makes people "feel better" (at least initially), but no one would suggest using heroin to treat a sick person.

- Marijuana use causes precancerous changes in the body similar to those caused by tobacco use. Smoking pot delivers 3 to 5 times the amount of tars and carbon monoxide into the body. It also damages pulmonary immunity and impairs oxygen diffusion. How could changes such as these be good for someone dying of cancer or AIDS?

4. *State initiatives*

- Voters at the state and local levels want to make decisions that are appropriate for their communities, but to do so they must have accurate information.

- Well-financed and organized campaigns have contributed to the misperception that marijuana is harmless or may even have health benefits.

- These campaigns are led not by medical professionals or patients-rights groups, but by pro-drug donors and organizations in a cynical attempt to exploit the suffering of sick people.

5. *The European experience*

- The "nirvana" offered by the Dutch example is extremely dubious; in fact, the Dutch government is now reconsidering its laws and policies regarding drugs.

- Increased availability of marijuana leads to increased use of this and other drugs, and it creates additional problems as well.

- After coffee shops started selling marijuana and use of the drug became normalized, marijuana use between 1984 and 1996 nearly tripled—from 15 percent to 44 percent—among 18- to 20-year-old Dutch youth.

- While our nation's consumption of cocaine has decreased by 70 percent over the past 15 years, cocaine consumption in Europe (primarily Western Europe) has increased.

6. *Drug testing in schools*

- Marijuana use affects the growth and development of young minds; it can inhibit students' ability to concentrate and retain information during the critical learning years.

- Student drug testing can be an important tool in preventing and treating youth drug use.

- It is important for parents, school officials, and community leaders to examine the nature and extent of their youth drug problem to determine if testing is appropriate for their schools.

- The goal of school-based drug testing is not to trap and punish students who do drugs. Rather, it is to prevent drug dependence and to help drug-using students stop and find treatment before the problem gets worse.

- According to the *Journal of Adolescent Health*, a school in Oregon that drug-tested student-athletes had a rate of drug use that was one-fourth that of a comparable school with no drug-testing policy.

- After two years of a drug-testing program, Hunterdon Central Regional High School in New Jersey saw significant reductions in 20 of 28 drug-use categories. Cocaine use by seniors, for example, dropped from 13 percent to only 4 percent.

- Testing provides a way for teens to resist peer pressure.

- Testing helps prevent drug use at a critical time in young people's lives. Research shows a strong link between drug dependence and the age of initiation. If people can be prevented from using drugs as teenagers, their chances of experiencing drug problems as adults are greatly diminished.

The Negative Consequences of Marijuana Use

National Institute on Drug Abuse

The National Institute on Drug Abuse (NIDA) is a government agency affiliated with the U.S. Department of Health and Human Services. The following NIDA research report surveys a number of recent scientific studies to underscore the widespread scope of marijuana use in the United States today, particularly among adolescents and young adults. The report documents the short- and long-term physical effects associated with smoking marijuana and demonstrates how the drug's persistent use can have a detrimental effect on the user's school, work, and social life.

What Is Marijuana?

Marijuana—often called *pot, grass, reefer, weed, herb, mary jane,* or *mj*—is a greenish-gray mixture of the dried, shredded leaves, stems, seeds, and flowers of *Cannabis sativa,* the hemp plant. Most users smoke marijuana in hand-rolled cigarettes called *joints,* among other names; some use pipes or water pipes called *bongs.* Marijuana cigars called *blunts* have also become popular. To make blunts, users slice open cigars and replace the tobacco with marijuana, often combined with another drug, such as crack cocaine. Marijuana also is used to brew tea and is sometimes mixed into foods.

The major active chemical in marijuana is delta-9-tetrahydrocannabinol (THC), which causes the mind-altering effects of marijuana intoxication. The amount of THC (which is also the psychoactive ingredient in hashish) determines the potency and, therefore, the effects of marijuana. Between 1980 and 1997, the amount of THC in marijuana available in the United States rose dramatically.

National Institute on Drug Abuse, "Marijuana Abuse," July 2005.

What Is the Scope of Marijuana Use in the United States?

Marijuana is the Nation's most commonly used illicit drug. More than 94 million Americans (40 percent) age 12 and older have tried marijuana at least once, according to the 2003 National Survey on Drug Use and Health (NSDUH).

Marijuana use is widespread among adolescents and young adults. The percentage of middle school students who reported using marijuana increased throughout the early 1990s. In the past few years, according to the 2004 Monitoring the Future Survey, an annual survey of drug use among the Nation's middle and high school students, illicit drug use by 8th-, 10th-, and 12th-graders has leveled off. Still, in 2004, 16 percent of 8th-graders reported that they had tried marijuana, and 6 percent were current users (defined as having used the drug in the 30 days preceding the survey). Among 10th-graders, 35 percent had tried marijuana sometime in their lives, and 16 percent were current users. As would be expected, rates of use among 12th-graders were higher still. Forty-six percent had tried marijuana at some time, and 20 percent were current users.

The Drug Abuse Warning Network (DAWN), a system for monitoring the health impact of drugs, estimated that, in 2002, marijuana was a contributing factor in over 119,000 emergency department (ED) visits in the United States, with about 15 percent of the patients between the ages of 12 and 17, and almost two-thirds male.

In 2002, the National Institute of Justice's Arrestee Drug Abuse Monitoring (ADAM) Program, which collects data on the number of adult arrestees testing positive for various drugs, found that, on average, 41 percent of adult male arrestees and 27 percent of adult female arrestees tested positive for marijuana. On average, 57 percent of juvenile male and 32 percent of juvenile female arrestees tested positive for marijuana.

NIDA's Community Epidemiology Work Group (CEWG), a network of researchers that tracks trends in the nature and patterns of drug use in major U.S. cities, consistently reports that marijuana frequently is combined with other drugs, such as crack cocaine, PCP, formaldehyde, and codeine cough syrup, sometimes without the user being aware of it. Thus, the risks associated with marijuana use may be compounded by the risks of added drugs, as well.

How Does Marijuana Affect the Brain?

Scientists have learned a great deal about how THC acts in the brain to produce its many effects. When someone smokes marijuana, THC rapidly passes from the lungs into the bloodstream, which carries the chemical to organs throughout the body, including the brain. In the brain, THC connects to specific sites called *cannabinoid receptors* on nerve cells and thereby influences the activity of those cells. Some brain areas have many cannabinoid receptors; others have few or none. Many cannabinoid receptors are found in the parts of the brain that influence pleasure, memory, thought, concentration, sensory and time perception, and coordinated movement.

What Are the Acute Effects of Marijuana Use?

When marijuana is smoked, its effects begin immediately after the drug enters the brain and last from 1 to 3 hours. If marijuana is consumed in food or drink, the short-term effects begin more slowly, usually in 1/2 to 1 hour, and last longer, for as long as 4 hours. Smoking marijuana deposits several times more THC into the blood than does eating or drinking the drug.

Within a few minutes after inhaling marijuana smoke, an individual's heart begins beating more rapidly, the bronchial passages relax and become enlarged, and blood vessels in the eyes expand, making the eyes look red. The heart rate, normally 70 to 80 beats per minute, may increase by 20 to 50 beats per minute or, in some cases, even double. This effect can be greater if other drugs are taken with marijuana.

As THC enters the brain, it causes a user to feel euphoric—or "high"—by acting in the brain's reward system, areas of the brain that respond to stimuli such as food and drink as well as most drugs of abuse. THC activates the reward system in the same way that nearly all drugs of abuse do, by stimulating brain cells to release the chemical dopamine.

A marijuana user may experience pleasant sensations, colors and sounds may seem more intense, and time appears to pass very slowly. The user's mouth feels dry, and he or she may suddenly become very hungry and thirsty. His or her hands may tremble and grow cold. The euphoria passes after awhile, and then the user may feel sleepy or depressed. Occasionally, marijuana use produces anxiety, fear, distrust, or panic.

Heavy marijuana use impairs a person's ability to form memories, recall events . . . and shift attention from one thing to another. THC also disrupts coordination and balance by binding to receptors in the cerebellum and basal ganglia, parts of the brain that regulate balance, posture, coordination of movement, and reaction time. Through its effects on the brain and body, marijuana intoxication can cause accidents. Studies show that approximately 6 to 11 percent of fatal accident victims test positive for THC. In many of these cases, alcohol is detected as well.

In a study conducted by the National Highway Traffic Safety Administration, a moderate dose of marijuana alone was shown to impair driving performance; however, the effects of even a low dose of marijuana combined with alcohol were markedly greater than for either drug alone. Driving indices measured included reaction time, visual search frequency (driver checking side streets), and the ability to perceive and/or respond to changes in the relative velocity of other vehicles.

Marijuana users who have taken high doses of the drug may experience acute toxic psychosis, which includes hallucinations, delusions, and depersonalization—a loss of the sense of personal identity, or self-recognition. Although the specific causes of these symptoms remain unknown, they appear to occur more frequently when a high dose of cannabis is consumed in food or drink rather than smoked.

How Does Marijuana Use Affect Physical Health?

Marijuana use has been shown to increase users' difficulty in trying to quit smoking tobacco. This was reported in a study comparing smoking cessation in adults who smoked both marijuana and tobacco with those who smoked only tobacco. The relationship between marijuana use and continued smoking was particularly strong in those who smoked marijuana daily at the time of the initial interview, 13 years prior to the followup interview.

A study of 450 individuals found that people who smoke marijuana frequently but do not smoke tobacco have more health problems and miss more days of work than nonsmokers do. Many of the extra sick days used by the marijuana smokers in the study were for respiratory illnesses.

Even infrequent marijuana use can cause burning and stinging of the mouth and throat, often accompanied by a heavy cough. Someone who smokes marijuana regularly may have many of the same respiratory problems that tobacco smokers do, such as daily cough and phlegm production, more frequent acute chest illnesses, a heightened risk of lung infections, and a greater tendency toward obstructed airways.

Cancer of the respiratory tract and lungs may also be promoted by marijuana smoke. A study comparing 173 cancer patients and 176 healthy individuals produced strong evidence that smoking marijuana increases the likelihood of developing cancer of the head or neck, and that the more marijuana smoked, the greater the increase. A statistical analysis of the data suggested that marijuana smoking doubled or tripled the risk of these cancers.

Marijuana has the potential to promote cancer of the lungs and other parts of the respiratory tract because it contains irritants and carcinogens. In fact, marijuana smoke contains 50 percent to 70 percent more carcinogenic hydrocarbons than does tobacco smoke. It also produces high levels of an enzyme that converts certain hydrocarbons into their carcinogenic form, levels that may accelerate the changes that ultimately produce malignant cells. Marijuana users usually inhale more deeply and hold their breath longer than tobacco smokers do, which increases the lungs' exposure to carcinogenic smoke. These facts suggest that, puff for puff, smoking marijuana may increase the risk of cancer more than smoking tobacco does.

Some adverse health effects caused by marijuana may occur because THC impairs the immune system's ability to fight off infectious diseases and cancer. In laboratory experiments that exposed animal and human cells to THC or other marijuana ingredients, the normal disease-preventing reactions of many of the key types of immune cells were inhibited. In other studies, mice exposed to THC or related substances were more likely than unexposed mice to develop bacterial infections and tumors.

One study has indicated that a person's risk of heart attack during the first hour after smoking marijuana is four times his or her usual risk. The researchers suggest that a heart attack might occur, in part, because marijuana raises blood pressure and heart rate and reduces the oxygen-carrying capacity of blood.

How Does Marijuana Use Affect School, Work, and Social Life?

Students who smoke marijuana get lower grades and are less likely to graduate from high school, compared with their non-smoking peers.

Workers who smoke marijuana are more likely than their coworkers to have problems on the job. Several studies have associated workers' marijuana smoking with increased absences, tardiness, accidents, workers' compensation claims, and job turnover. A study among postal workers found that employees who tested positive for marijuana on a pre-employment urine drug test had 55 percent more industrial accidents, 85 percent more injuries, and a 75 percent increase in absenteeism compared with those who tested negative for marijuana use.

Depression, anxiety, and personality disturbances are all associated with marijuana use. Research clearly demonstrates that marijuana use has the potential to cause problems in daily life or make a person's existing problems worse. Because marijuana compromises the ability to learn and remember information, the more a person uses marijuana the more he or she is likely to fall behind in accumulating intellectual, job, or social skills. In one study of cognition, adults were matched on the basis of their performance in the 4th-grade on the Iowa Test of Basic Skills. They were evaluated on a number of cognitive measures including the 12th-grade version of the Iowa Test. Those who were heavy marijuana smokers scored significantly lower on mathematical skills and verbal expression than nonsmokers.

Moreover, research has shown that marijuana's adverse impact on memory and learning can last for days or weeks after the acute effects of the drug wear off. For example, a study of 129 college students found that among heavy users of marijuana—those who smoked the drug at least 27 of the preceding 30 days—critical skills related to attention, memory, and learning were significantly impaired, even after they had not used the drug for at least 24 hours. The heavy marijuana users in the study had more trouble sustaining and shifting their attention and in registering, organizing, and using information than did the study participants who had used marijuana no more than 3 of the previous 30 days. As a result, someone who smokes marijuana once daily may be functioning at a reduced intellectual level all of the time. More recently, the same researchers showed that a group of long-term heavy marijuana users' ability to recall words from a list was impaired 1 week following cessation of marijuana use, but returned to normal by 4 weeks. An implication of this finding is that even after long-term heavy marijuana use, if an individual quits marijuana use, some cognitive abilities may be recovered.

Another study produced additional evidence that marijuana's effects on the brain can cause cumulative deterioration of critical life skills in the long run. Researchers gave students a battery of tests measuring problem-solving and emotional skills in 8th-grade and again in 12th-grade. The results showed that the students who were already drinking alcohol plus smoking marijuana in 8th grade started off slightly behind their peers, but that the distance separating these two groups grew significantly by their senior year in high school. The analysis linked marijuana use, independently of alcohol use, to reduced capacity for self-reinforcement, a group of psychological skills that enable individuals to maintain confidence and persevere in the pursuit of goals.

Marijuana users themselves report poor outcomes on a variety of measures of life satisfaction and achievement. A recent study compared current and former long-term heavy users of marijuana with a control group who reported smoking cannabis at least once in their lives, but not more than 50 times. Despite similar education and incomes in their families of origin, significant differences were found in educational attainment and income between heavy users and the control group: fewer of the cannabis users completed college and more had household incomes of less than $30,000. When asked how marijuana affected their cognitive abilities, career achievements, social lives, and physical and mental health, the overwhelming majority of heavy cannabis users reported the drug's deleterious effect on all of these measures.

Can Marijuana Use During Pregnancy Harm the Baby?

Research has shown that some babies born to women who used marijuana during their pregnancies display altered responses to visual stimuli, increased tremulousness, and a high-pitched cry, which may indicate problems with neurological development. During the preschool years, marijuana-exposed children have been observed to perform tasks involving sustained attention and memory more poorly than nonexposed children do. In the school years, these children are more likely to exhibit deficits in problem-solving skills, memory, and the ability to remain attentive.

Is Marijuana Use Addictive?

Long-term marijuana use can lead to addiction for some people; that is, they use the drug compulsively even though it often interferes with family, school, work, and recreational activities. According to the 2003 National Survey on Drug Use and Health (NSDUH), an estimated 21.6 million Americans aged 12 or older were classified with substance dependence or abuse (9.1 percent of the total population). Of the estimated 6.9 million Americans classified with dependence on or abuse of illicit drugs, 4.2 million were dependent on or abused marijuana. In 2002, 15 percent of people entering drug abuse treatment programs reported that marijuana was their primary drug of abuse.

Along with craving, withdrawal symptoms can make it hard for long-term marijuana smokers to stop using the drug.

People trying to quit report irritability, difficulty sleeping, and anxiety. They also display increased aggression on psychological tests, peaking approximately 1 week after they last used the drug.

In addition to its addictive liability, research indicates that early exposure to marijuana can increase the likelihood of a lifetime of subsequent drug problems. A recent study of over 300 fraternal and identical twin pairs, who differed on whether or not they used marijuana before the age of 17, found that those who had used marijuana early had elevated rates of other drug use and drug problems later on, compared with their twins, who did not use marijuana before age 17. This study re-emphasizes the importance of primary prevention by showing that early drug initiation is associated with increased risk of later drug problems, and it provides more evidence for why preventing marijuana experimentation during adolescence could have an impact on preventing addiction.

What Treatments Are Available for Marijuana Abusers?

Treatment programs directed solely at marijuana abuse are rare, partly because many who use marijuana do so in combination with other drugs, such as cocaine and alcohol. However, with more people seeking help to control marijuana abuse, research has focused on ways to overcome problems with abuse of this drug.

One study of adult marijuana users found comparable benefits from a 14-session cognitive-behavioral group treatment and a 2-session individual treatment that included motivational interviewing and advice on ways to reduce marijuana use. Participants were mostly men in their early thirties who had smoked marijuana daily for over 10 years. By increasing patients' awareness of what triggers their marijuana use, both treatments sought to help them devise avoidance strategies. Use, dependence symptoms, and psychosocial problems decreased for at least 1 year after both treatments. About 30 percent of users were abstinent during the last 3-month followup period. Another study suggests that giving patients vouchers for abstaining from marijuana can improve outcomes. Vouchers can be redeemed for such goods as movie passes, sports equipment, or vocational training.

No medications are now available to treat marijuana abuse. However, recent discoveries about the workings of THC receptors have raised the possibility that scientists may eventually develop a medication that will block THC's intoxicating effects. Such a medication might be used to prevent relapse to marijuana abuse by reducing or eliminating its appeal.

Where Can I Get Further Scientific Information About Marijuana?

To learn more about marijuana and other drugs of abuse, contact the National Clearinghouse for Alcohol and Drug Information (NCADI) at 1-800-729-6686. Information specialists are available to help you locate information and resources.

Fact sheets, including *InfoFacts*, on the health effects of marijuana, other drugs of abuse, and other drug abuse topics are available on the NIDA Web site (www.drugabuse.gov), and can be ordered free of charge in English and Spanish from NCADI at www.health.org.

Beneficial Effects of Marijuana as a Medical Prescription

Rudolph J. Gerber

An advocate for the medical use of marijuana, Rudolph J. Gerber cites a number of independent studies that endorse the therapeutic benefits of using pot to treat symptoms associated with AIDS, cancer, multiple sclerosis, Tourette's syndrome, and anxiety. In the following article Gerber discusses what he believes are the negligible short- and long-term health effects of smoking pot; contends that the drug is neither addictive nor toxic like tobacco, alcohol, or many over-the-counter prescriptions; and points out that there is no record anywhere of fatality or overdose related to marijuana use. Further, Gerber presents evidence from several sources to prove that marijuana is not a gateway drug that introduces users to more addictive narcotics. According to Gerber, ingrained cultural biases and the federal government's misguided, unremitting policy of prohibition have prevented impartial, independent scientific research programs, which could, in turn, lead to the legalization and prescription use of marijuana for medical purposes.

Pot's Health Benefits

Drug sociologist Lynn Zimmer and narcotics researcher John P. Morgan have found significant health benefits from pot. For glaucoma, marijuana reduces the fluid pressure in the eyes that causes irreversible damage to vision. For AIDS patients, marijuana addresses their immunosuppression and the danger posed by lung irritants and fungal illnesses such as aspergillosis. Many AIDS patients with treatment-induced nausea, appetite loss, and wasting syndrome claim that marijuana saved their lives by motivating them to eat.

Almost half the oncologists in a 1990 study recommended pot to their patients. By then, pot's core ingredient was already legal: Dronabinol, marketed as Marinol, a synthetic THC [delta-9-tetrahydrocannabinol, a major active chemical in marijuana] compound using the active ingredient in pot, continues as a legal drug in pill form prescribed for nausea, depression, and spasticity. The federal taboo on pot thus acquires an Orwellian irony: prohibition of the same substance the government has previously approved under a different name.

Marinol, a 1985 creation by Unimed Pharmaceutical and selling for about $15 per 10-mg pill, acts as a poor substitute for marijuana because doses cannot be titrated as precisely. Marinol can cost upward of $500 per dosage or between $600 and $1,000 per month, considerably more than even high-quality marijuana. Opponents of medical marijuana claim that all medicines need approval by the FDA, but drug companies have little incentive to overcome the regulatory and financial obstacles for a plant that cannot be patented.

As of 2001, the capsule form of Marinol was more cumbersome than smoked marijuana in delivering pain relief. Here are the major differences between the two:

- The onset of relief from the capsule takes an hour or more: smoking takes effect within minutes.

- The one-hour lag time means that oral dosage by capsules is difficult to adjust and monitor; a patient can cease or continue smoking in response to minute-to-minute results.

- Oral THC is metabolized through the liver, neutralizing more than 90 percent of the chemical; smoking pot delivers the THC directly to the bloodstream.

- An oral dose lasts six unpredictable hours, with variable effects; in the same patient, smoking pot lasts a more manageable and predicable hour or two.

- Some patients whose livers metabolize the synthetic delta-9 THC into a more psychoactive 11-hydroxy-THC get more stoned on a metabolite.

- According to 2003 figures, a moderate Marinol regimen can cost about $1,000 a month while the cost of smoking quality marijuana for a month is much less and would be negligible if medical cultivation became legal.

- Compared with most painkillers and sedatives based on opiates, medical marijuana reduces pain without causing physical addiction, nor does it carry the risk to patients of developing tolerance to the extent of requiring increasing doses.

Many approved non-THC alternatives to pot present serious side effects. The antiemetics Compazine and Decadron pose a great risk of liver damage. Marijuana is safer than many over-the-counter drugs. Asked to evaluate the medical benefits of marijuana, the DEA's [Drug Enforcement Administration] own administrative judge Francis L. Young declared in a ninety-page decision in 1988—impoliticly, from the DEA's point of view—that marijuana was "one of the safest therapeutically active substances known to man."

The DEA's politicians concluded otherwise. In 1992, brushing aside the ruling while ridiculing medical marijuana as a dangerous and "cruel hoax," DEA officials slammed the door on Judge Young's findings by reversing his decision on unstated political grounds. Thus arose a continuing anomaly: the more costly, more cumbersome, less effective drug Marinol remained legal while the more efficient, less costly same drug under the suspect name of marijuana remained criminal.

Pain-killing Abilities

Ironically, this excoriated drug also has pain-killing powers. Animal studies by research groups at the University of California—San Francisco, the University of Michigan, and Brown University have shown that a group of potent cannabinoids, including the active ingredient in marijuana, relieves several kinds of pain, including the inflammation of arthritis as well as severe forms of chronic pain. In 1997, a panel of experts convened by the National Institute of Health's Society for Neuroscience reported at its annual meeting that the active chemicals in marijuana cause a direct beneficial effect on pain signals in the central nervous system. Unlike opiate-based painkillers, pot's painkillers are not addictive; continued use does not develop tolerance.

Although the government continues to claim that the vast majority of American physicians remain opposed to the medical use of marijuana, a 1990 survey of oncologists by researchers at the Kennedy School of Government at Harvard revealed that nearly half of those who responded said that they would prescribe pot to cancer patients if it were legal to do so.

Despite some medical folklore about the negative therapeutic effects of smoked marijuana, studies indicate that the active chemicals in marijuana directly mitigate pain signals and that marijuana, unlike prescribable opiate-based drugs, carries no risk of patients developing a tolerance requiring increasing doses. For the government to prosecute physicians for recommending medical marijuana denies viable medical treatment, perhaps the best existing treatment, for patients suffering from debilitating illnesses. Indeed, such prosecutions contradict the government's original rationale for setting up its Compassionate User Program.

Safety Comparisons

Though it remains criminal, pot offers a vastly superior safety record in comparison to legal drugs. Although the misuse of over-the-counter medications such as aspirin, acetaminophen, ephedra, and antihistamines each year kills thousands of Americans, pot is one of the few drugs that has yet to cause a fatality. Nor is there any known fatal dosage. It is that rare drug without risk of overdose—except to force-fed monkeys.

Harvard's Lester Grinspoon has shown that marijuana can relieve nausea associated with chemotherapy, prevent blindness induced by glaucoma, serve as an appetite stimulant for AIDS patients, act an antiepileptic, ward off asthma attacks and migraine headaches, alleviate chronic pain, and reduce the muscle spasticity that accompanies multiple sclerosis, cerebral palsy, and paraplegia. As of 2002, the federal government remains deaf and blind to Grinspoon's research as well as to the statistical differences in mortality between pot and legal drugs. For the past quarter century, and particularly in the Reagan, Bush Sr., and Clinton administrations, drug policy wonks focused more on seeking marijuana's professed but illusive ill effects than in trying to lessen the country's dependence on far more detrimental drugs such as alcohol and tobacco.

Pot's medical benefits have eminent references. The well-known Harvard geologist Stephen Jay Gould developed abdominal cancer in the 1980s, suffering such intense nausea from intravenous chemotherapy that he came to dread chemotherapy with an "almost perverse intensity." The treatment, he remembered, acted "worse than the disease itself." Initially reluctant to smoke marijuana, Gould eventually found it "the greatest boost I received in all my years of treatment." "It is beyond my comprehension," he concluded, "and I fancy myself able to comprehend a lot, including such nonsense that any humane person would withhold such a beneficial substance from people in such great need simply because others use it for different purposes."

Recent Pot Research

The 1990s saw increased medical studies on the effects of medical marijuana. A 1997 study performed on experimental animals at the University of California found that THC effectively relieved pain without the adverse side effects associated with opiates. In 1995, the British medical journal *Lancet* reported research showing that pot is safer than alcohol or tobacco; it editorialized that smoking pot, "even long term, is not harmful to health," and added that more recent research showed it to "reduce the pain and muscle stiffness of multiple sclerosis." In 1999, the *American Journal of Psychiatry* reported German research showing that THC in pot successfully treated Tourette's syndrome. The National Academy of Sciences reported in its 1998 *Proceedings* that marijuana protects brain cells during a stroke. In early 2000, researchers in England reported pot effective in controlling the muscle spasms of multiple sclerosis.

Given these medical benefits, some doctors have become willing to recommend marijuana for a variety of ailments. In response to a DEA inference that only fringe doctors would recommend marijuana as an antiemetic agent, a random sample of members of the American Society of Clinical Oncology interviewed by Harvard scientists in 1990 revealed that of the more than 1,000 oncologists responding, about 44 percent admitted that they had already recommended marijuana to at least one patient. Further, those responding indicated that they believed pot to be more effective than oral dronabinol.

Memory Benefits

Not the least of marijuana's benefits is a modern version of the Lotus Eaters' visit to Lethe in Homer's *Odyssey* selective forgetfulness. Allyn Howlett, the St. Louis University medical researcher who discovered a specific receptor for THC in the brain, has shown that cannabis models the work of natural neurotransmitters such as serotonin, dopamine, and the endorphins. Like these other transmitters, pot's THC contributes to anxiety relief by softening painful memories. "It's a palliative that enables us to get up and back to work on Monday mornings," writes drug researcher Michael Pollan.

Almost identical results have come from German research in 2002 at the Max Planck Institute of Psychiatry in Munich. There neurological researchers found that pot's cannabinoids can wipe out bad memories by dampening nerve cell action contributing to the anxiety stemming from remembered bad experiences. Cannabinoids bind to the brain's chemical receptors to create a feeling of euphoria as they mask painful memories, a result comparable to that achieved by Xanax, Wellbutrin, Prozac, Valium, and a host of similar legally permitted drugs.

Pot, Tobacco, and Alcohol

A 1991 U.S. Department of Health and Human Services report to Congress stated: "Given the large population of marijuana users and the infrequent reports of medical problems from stopping use, tolerance and dependence are not major issues at present." Indeed, no one can be very certain what "marijuana treatment" would look like. "Long-term heavy marijuana use does not produce the severe or grossly debilitating impairment of memory, attention, and cognitive function found with chronic heavy alcohol use," says the British medical journal *Lancet*. Only a small minority of users eventually smoke enough of it for a long period to suffer impairments matching those of prolonged tobacco use. Jailing such users dashes with the government's approach to the more harmful effects of tobacco and alcohol, whose abuses do not generate alerts, arrests, forfeitures, or convictions.

In 2001, two of the weed's strongest political critics, Republicans Mitch McConnell of Kentucky and Bob Barr of Georgia, tried without success to ban all medical use of marijuana and to increase penalties for its use. "All civilized countries in the world," according to Barr, "are under assault by drug proponents seeking to enslave citizens." Both lawmakers come from tobacco-producing states. Despite the fact that over 400,000 citizens of this country die each year from tobacco, these two anti-addiction crusaders focused their legislative energies on demonizing marijuana, a drug that, unlike their homegrown tobacco, has never caused a single death.

In its March 19, 2002, issue, the British medical journal *New Scientist* reported that a single glass of wine impairs driving more than smoking one marijuana joint. The report refutes a common misconception that weed smoking poses as great a threat to safe driving as does alcohol. Conducted by the Transport Research Laboratory in Crowthorne, Berkshire, the study showed that marijuana affected just one test category, the ability of drivers to follow the middle of the road while driving a figure eight loop. Drivers who drank the equivalent of a glass of wine fared much worse on the task than did those who had smoked an entire joint. A similar California study of over 300 drivers in fatal accidents in that state focused on drivers who tested positive for pot but no other drug. Surprisingly, they were found to be half as likely to be responsible for accidents as those free of all substances.

National Institute of Medicine Report

The most exacting—and politically unwelcome—research findings on pot's medical effects appeared in a nonpartisan March 1999 report from our government's Institute of Medicine. Entitled *Marijuana and Medicine; Assessing the Science Base*, the 250-page report, commissioned by none other than drug czar General McCaffrey, found that smoking marijuana effectively treated nausea and severe weight loss associated with AIDS and cancer treatment. To improve its medical effects, the Institute urged development of new delivery mechanisms, such as bronchial inhalers used by asthma patients. The report recommended that pot be provided, under dose supervision for a limited time, to patients not responding to other medical therapies.

The institute's conclusion causing the biggest stir, however, impacted policy more than medicine. The eleven medical researchers found no evidence that ill persons' marijuana use increased illicit drug use in other populations. Contrary to Ms. Schuchard, Bill Bennett, John Walters, and other imaginative medicine men and women, these independent medical researchers found marijuana does not act as a gateway to more dangerous narcotics like cocaine and heroin. The institute's $896,000 study concluded that the future of pot's medicinal use lay not in lighting up joints, since smoking pot can lead to lung damage and low-birth-weight babies, but in the development of safer delivery systems, like a vaporizer or patch to more effectively deliver pot's active ingredients to sick users.

The Institute of Medicine report suggested interim solutions for some sick and dying patients unable to benefit from approved painkillers and antinausea drugs. "There are limited circumstances in which we see recommending smoked marijuana for medical uses," wrote Dr. John Benson Jr., former dean of Oregon Health Sciences University, one of the two principal medical investigators. According to the report, thousands of patients with nausea and vomiting from chemotherapy could benefit from marijuana in carefully controlled trials.

Not surprisingly, the Institute's report touched a sensitive nerve within the Clinton administration, especially with its suggestion that the federal government commit to doing medical marijuana research to deliver pot's benefits for certain classes of sick patients. In the meantime, the researchers recommended, the government ought to reopen the "compassionate user" medical marijuana program suspended by the Bush administration in 1992 (because of "the wrong message") to provide legal access to medical marijuana to seriously ill persons.

In a muted response to this government research, McCaffrey quoted only the report's conclusion that the future of cannabinoid drugs "lies not in smoked marijuana, but in chemically defined drugs that act on . . . human physiology." He then called for still more pot research, thus continuing the government's longstanding search for some ill effect to justify pot's prior prohibition, a task made more difficult by this latest government report denying, again, the very ills drug warriors sought.

In May 1999, shortly after the Institute of Medicine report, and in response to it, the Department of Health and Human Services released new guidelines on "Procedures for the Provision of Marijuana for Medical Research," to allow the National Institute on Drug Abuse [NIDA] to sell government pot plants from its Mississippi pot farm to privately funded scientists for "scientifically valid investigations" preapproved by NIDA. The new guidelines contained numerous impediments to medical marijuana research and continued to deny lawful access to medical marijuana by seriously ill patients. The guidelines explicitly rejected the Institute's recommendation that the government expand its compassionate user program.

In December 2001, the Drug Enforcement Administration announced limited research, to begin in 2002, on the medical uses of marijuana for neuropathy and muscle rigidity. The new research did not make it legal for doctors to provide pot as medicine to their patients but allowed pot for limited use only in scientific experiments. Approval for this research ended a two-decade-long federal de facto prohibition on medical research on marijuana. One of the principal researchers, Dr. Donald Abrams of the University of California, noted that the important factors in getting the new research approved were successful medical marijuana referenda in Arizona and California in 1996.

Rand Institute Study

In December 2002, the Rand Drug Policy Research Center in California published a lengthy study casting further doubt on claims that marijuana acts as a medical gateway to harder drugs. According to Rand, an alternative, simpler, and more compelling explanation accounts for the pattern of transitioning to hard-drug use. Associations between marijuana and hard drugs result from known differences in the ages at which youth have opportunities to use marijuana and hard drugs and known variations in their willingness to try any drugs. Rand researchers tested the gateway theory by creating a mathematical model simulating drug use. The model's rates of pot use and hard-drug use matched youthful drug-use data.

Without use of a gateway effect, the model produced patterns of drug use remarkably similar to the real-world data, showing the marijuana gateway theory to be an unnecessary construct for explaining hard-drug use. Rand's chief researcher Andrew Morral concluded that the study "suggests that policies aimed at reducing or eliminating marijuana availability are unlikely to make any dent in the hard drug problem." He added that "Enforcement resources used against heroin and cocaine if used against marijuana could have the unintended effect of worsening heroin and cocaine use," as seems to have occurred toward the end of the Reagan presidency.

The National Institute of Medicine and Rand studies helped to convert some former drug warriors. President Reagan's former drug czar Charles Schuster responded to the Rand study by saying he could "only hope that this report will be read with objectivity and evaluated on its scientific merits, not reflexively rejected because it violates most policy makers' belief."

"Less of a Threat"

While marijuana is not harmless, its harms pale compared to over-the counter drugs and euphoriants like alcohol and tobacco, and common pacifiers like Valium and Xanax. In the view of the British medical journal *Lancet*, an objective person can reliably judge pot "less of a threat than alcohol or tobacco." Merely on the medical evidence alone, according to *Lancet,* "moderate indulgence in cannabis presents little ill-effect on health." Drug czar McCaffrey's sponsored Institute of Medicine report in March 1999 reached similar conclusions about the medical benefits of marijuana and the absence of any evidence that it "primes" its users to move on to harder drugs.

University researcher Mitch Earleywine, the author of America's definitive compendium of pot medical research, has reached parallel conclusions in reviewing all the current medical data. Medical research, he finds, shows that marijuana's medical harms approximate those of tobacco when it is used with equal frequency, which it rarely is because its effects are more immediate and less toxic. Pot's medical benefits extend to nausea, appetite stimulation, convulsion control, relief from glaucoma pressure and pain, and memory softening. It is neither as toxic nor as fatal as our legal drugs alcohol and tobacco, nor is it a gateway to harder drugs.

CHAPTER 2

The Medical Marijuana Debate

The FDA Joins the Medical Marijuana Debate

Gardiner Harris

*The Food and Drug Administration (FDA) is a federal govern-
ment agency that continuously monitors the safety of all food,
cosmetics, and medicines that have been approved for public
consumption in the United States. In the following* New York
Times *piece, Gardiner Harris considers the scientific and political implications of the release of a 2006 FDA report which dis-
misses the conclusions reached by the Institute of Medicine—a
highly regarded scientific advisory committee—that smoked
marijuana can provide medical relief for some AIDS and cancer
patients.*

Health Agency Joins Debate

The Food and Drug Administration said Thursday [April
20, 2006] that "no sound scientific studies" supported the
medical use of marijuana, contradicting a 1999 review by a
panel of highly regarded scientists.

The announcement inserts the health agency into yet another fierce political fight.

Susan Bro, an agency spokeswoman, said Thursday's statement resulted from a past combined review by federal drug
enforcement, regulatory and research agencies that concluded
"smoked marijuana has no currently accepted or proven medical use in the United States and is not an approved medical
treatment."

Ms. Bro said the agency issued the statement in response
to numerous inquiries from Capitol Hill but would probably
do nothing to enforce it.

"Any enforcement based on this finding would need to be by D.E.A. since this falls outside of F.D.A.'s regulatory authority," she said.

Federal Government and Some States at Odds

Eleven states have legalized medicinal use of marijuana, but the Drug Enforcement Administration and the director of national drug control policy, John P. Walters, have opposed those laws.

A Supreme Court decision last year allowed the federal government to arrest anyone using marijuana, even for medical purposes and even in states that have legalized its use.

Congressional opponents and supporters of medical marijuana use have each tried to enlist the F.D.A. to support their views. Representative Mark Souder, Republican of Indiana and a fierce opponent of medical marijuana initiatives, proposed legislation two years ago that would have required the food and drug agency to issue an opinion on the medicinal properties of marijuana.

Mr. Souder believes that efforts to legalize medicinal uses of marijuana are a front for efforts to legalize all uses of it, said Martin Green, a spokesman for Mr. Souder.

Tom Riley, a spokesman for Mr. Walters, hailed the food and drug agency's statement, saying it would put to rest what he called "the bizarre public discussion" that has led to some legalization of medical marijuana.

Scientific Agency Sees Benefits to Medical Marijuana

The Food and Drug Administration statement directly contradicts a 1999 review by the Institute of Medicine, a part of the National Academy of Sciences, the nation's most prestigious scientific advisory agency. That review found marijuana to be "moderately well suited for particular conditions, such as chemotherapy-induced nausea and vomiting and AIDS wasting."

Dr. John Benson, co-chairman of the Institute of Medicine committee that examined the research into marijuana's effects, said in an interview that the statement on Thursday [by the FDA] and the combined review by other agencies were wrong.

The federal government "loves to ignore our report," said Dr. Benson, a professor of internal medicine at the University of Nebraska Medical Center. "They would rather it never happened."

Some scientists and legislators said the agency's statement about marijuana demonstrated that politics had trumped science.

"Unfortunately, this is yet another example of the F.D.A. making pronouncements that seem to be driven more by ideology than by science," said Dr. Jerry Avorn, a medical professor at Harvard Medical School.

Representative Maurice D. Hinchey, a New York Democrat who has sponsored legislation to allow medicinal uses of marijuana, said the statement reflected the influence of the Drug Enforcement Administration, which he said had long pressured the F.D.A. to help in its fight against marijuana.

A spokeswoman for the Drug Enforcement Administration referred questions to Mr. Walters's office.

The Food and Drug Administration's statement said state initiatives that legalize marijuana use were "inconsistent with efforts to ensure that medications undergo the rigorous scientific scrutiny of the F.D.A. approval process."

Government Discourages Research, Scientists Claim

But scientists who study the medical use of marijuana said in interviews that the federal government had actively discouraged research. Lyle E. Craker, a professor in the division of plant and soil sciences at the University of Massachusetts, said he submitted an application to the D.E.A. in 2001 to grow a small patch of marijuana to be used for research because government-approved marijuana, grown in Mississippi, was of poor quality.

In 2004, the drug enforcement agency turned Dr. Craker down. He appealed and is awaiting a judge's ruling. "The reason there's no good evidence is that they don't want an honest trial," Dr. Craker said.

Dr. Donald Abrams, a professor of clinical medicine at the University of California, San Francisco, said he has studied marijuana's medicinal effects for years but had been frustrated because the National Institutes of Health, the leading government medical research agency, had refused to finance such work.

With financing from the State of California, Dr. Abrams undertook what he said was a rigorous, placebo-controlled trial of marijuana smoking in H.I.V. patients who suffered from nerve pain. Smoking marijuana proved effective in ameliorating pain, Dr. Abrams said, but he said he was having trouble getting the study published.

"One wonders how anyone" could fulfill the Food and Drug Administration request for well-controlled trials to prove marijuana's benefits, he said.

Government-Sanctioned Alternatives

Marinol, a synthetic version of a marijuana component, is approved to treat anorexia associated with AIDS and the nausea and vomiting associated with cancer drug therapy.

GW Pharmaceutical, a British company, has received F.D.A. approval to test a sprayed extract of marijuana in humans. Called Sativex, the drug is made from marijuana and is approved for sale in Canada. Opponents of efforts to legalize marijuana for medicinal uses suggest that marijuana is a so-called gateway drug that often leads users to try more danger-ous drugs and to addiction.

But the Institute of Medicine report concluded there was no evidence that marijuana acted as a gateway to harder drugs. And it said there was no evidence that medical use of mari-juana would increase its use among the general population.

Dr. Daniele Piomelli, a professor of pharmacology at the University of California, Irvine, said he had "never met a sci-entist who would say that marijuana is either dangerous or useless."

Studies clearly show that marijuana has some benefits for some patients, Dr. Piomelli said.

"We all agree on that," he said.

The Case for Marijuana by Prescription

Clare Wilson

In the following article Clare Wilson points out that in some cases licensed medications do not provide relief for many patients afflicted by chronic pain, particularly those who suffer from multiple sclerosis, AIDS, or spinal injuries. She observes that despite anecdotal evidence suggesting that smoking marijuana helps to relieve pain, doctors cannot legally prescribe the illicit and unregulated drug to their patients. Historically, Wilson says, medical researchers have been thwarted by governmental agencies in their attempts to fund and implement clinical trials to determine the potential benefits of treating patients with marijuana. Recently, though, pharmaceutical entrepreneur Geoffrey Guy secured permission from British authorities to carry out medical trials on safe and consistent formulations of cannabis. As a result, Guy's company, GW Pharmaceuticals, has developed an under-the-tongue spray called Sativax—the first prescription pharmaceutical drug based on marijuana. Sativax is on the verge of being approved for use in Canada, Australia, and New Zealand.

"I have had patients commit suicide because they said life had no meaning for them any more," says William Notcutt, an anaesthetist at James Paget Hospital in Great Yarmouth, Norfolk, on England's east coast. Notcutt specialises in treating patients in severe long-term pain. The causes are varied, ranging from spinal injuries to multiple sclerosis, but most of the patients have one thing in common: existing medicines don't help them.

"It's not just the pain, it's also what it does to your life," Notcutt says. "You've lost your job, you have financial problems, your spouse is fed up. I hear these heart-rending stories of people whose lives are crap."

The Criminal Cure

If there is one thing more frustrating for a doctor than being unable to deal with a patient's problem, perhaps it is knowing that there is a drug that could help—but they are not allowed to prescribe it. For Notcutt that drug is cannabis. Many patients with difficult-to-treat conditions use cannabis to relieve their symptoms, but in most parts of the world that makes them criminals. Otherwise law-abiding citizens dislike having to get their treatments from drug dealers. And the quality of the medication they get that way is variable to say the least.

But in the next few weeks [February 2005] Canadian regulators will decide whether to approve an under-the-tongue cannabis spray called Sativex for multiple sclerosis (MS) patients. As the world's first prescription pharmaceutical made from marijuana, it would at last allow patients to get their therapy in a safe and consistent formulation. The product could become available in the UK in a year or so, and its British manufacturer, GW Pharmaceuticals, is expected to file for approval soon in Australia and New Zealand.

Sativex will not bring any miracle cures, and in countries like the US where official hostility to marijuana is ingrained, patients may have a longer wait for its benefits. All the same, the availability of a cannabis preparation as a prescription medicine will mark a milestone in a decades-long battle by doctors and patients for public acceptance of medical cannabis use.

A Long History of Healing

Marijuana use has a long history. For thousands of years, people have been harvesting the seeds for food and oil, and making rope from the fibres.

The plant is used in traditional medicine all over the world to relieve pain and muscle spasms, to prevent seizures and to aid sleep. It may also alleviate nausea—though it can sometimes trigger nausea in new users—and it can boost appetite.

But the drug is best known for its effects on the mind: it is an intoxicant that makes people feel happy and relaxed, and over the past century its recreational use has become increasingly popular in the west. Cannabis is not very addictive and its harmful effects are mainly on the lungs, from smoking. In some users it can trigger delusions and hallucinations, and there is debate about whether it can cause longer-term psychiatric problems in a small minority. In the early 20th century, most western governments responded to what they saw as the growing menace of marijuana by outlawing it.

As for medicinal use, cannabis came to be seen as an obsolete herbal remedy with unpredictable potency. It disappeared from the *US Pharmacopeia and National Formulary* in 1941, and the *British National Formulary* in 1971.

Formal Medical Research Begins

Until the late 1980s, when Notcutt began investigating the medicinal use of cannabis, research on the drug was focused mainly on establishing its dangers to people who used it recreationally, or its effects on animals.

Notcutt's interest grew out of his wish to find something new to deal with his patients' chronic pain. He found repeated references to the drug in historical medical texts on pain relief, and a growing body of research on animals showed that the main active chemical of cannabis, tetrahydrocannabinol (THC), bound to specific receptors in the brain.

In 1982 a form of synthetic THC had been licensed for relieving nausea after cancer chemotherapy, so Notcutt's first step was to investigate this for pain.

He began a small trial in his worst-affected patients, mostly people with spinal injuries. Some of them said THC helped; some of them said it made them feel dreadful. Others said it wasn't as good as the "real stuff." Thus Notcutt was introduced to the underground world of medical marijuana use. Even in sleepy Norfolk he found a small subculture of people who were getting what they viewed as an essential medicine from their local drug dealers.

Notcutt began seeing growing number of MS patients, who said cannabis relieved their pain and muscle "spasticity"—spasms and stiffness—and helped them sleep. The next step, Notcutt says, was to find a better way to give the patients what they wanted. In the early 1990s he and his team began exploring how they might carry out a clinical trial of cannabis.

They immediately ran into difficulties, because of the drug's illegal status and the resulting haphazard supply chain. "Are you going to use any old thing that comes off the Felixstowe docks?" he asks. "What's the quality, how do you standardise it?" They also failed to come up with a safe and effective way to administer the drug. Taken orally, marijuana's potency varies markedly and it doesn't become effective for at least an hour.

Smoke it, and you inhale a bunch of cancer-causing chemicals just as you do when smoking tobacco.

Research in the United States

In California, Donald Abrams, an HIV specialist at San Francisco General Hospital, was facing similar problems. He was interested in the possibility that cannabis could help people with AIDS stave off catastrophic weight loss. "They'd get loss of appetite and diarrhoea and just sort of waste away," Abrams says. "It was a terrible way to go." In 1992, synthetic THC was licensed for combating the nausea that is a symptom of AIDS, but, as with MS patients, many found marijuana more effective. Like the English patients, they faced supply problems. After a 70-year-old volunteer helper at his clinic was arrested for giving patients cannabis-laced brownies, Abrams decided to carry out a formal trial of marijuana.

If anything, he faced even stiffer opposition than Notcutt. In 1994 the team asked permission from the US Drug Enforcement Administration to obtain cannabis from a Dutch firm called Hortapharm but was turned down. They next approached the National Institute on Drug Abuse (NIDA), the only domestic body allowed to provide marijuana for research. Again they were rejected, partly because officials said they feared patients might sell their drugs on the street, and partly because the institute was more interested in investigating the harm from recreational cannabis use. A third proposal to NIDA, in 1996, was also turned down.

A Shift in Attitudes

By [1996], official attitudes in the UK were showing signs of becoming more favourable to medicinal marijuana. Paradoxically, this stemmed partly from anti-drug sentiment. Increasing numbers of MS patients using marijuana were ending up in court, and many were given light sentences or effectively let off. Concerned that this was bringing drug laws into disrepute, the government started to make positive if cautious noises about legalising medicinal cannabis if a pharmaceutical form of it could be developed.

At the same time, medical research into cannabis was gaining respectability globally as details began to emerge about the cannabinoids our own bodies produce. . . . But such research was almost entirely carried out by academics. What pharmaceutical firm would want to risk investing in such a politically controversial and financially uncertain field?

A Pharmaceutical Entrepreneur

Enter Geoffrey Guy, a businessman with a background in pharmaceuticals who was looking for his next venture. Cannabis's long history ruled out the normal route for making money from a drug by patenting it as a therapy. But Guy realised he could gain market exclusivity by developing a drug from cloned cannabis subspecies to which he owned the plant-breeders rights. Guy recalls that when he approached government officials for a licence to research his idea, they needed little convincing. "They were almost relieved that a company had turned up," he says. "I was pushing on a door that sprung open."

His new company, GW Pharmaceuticals, bought several strains of cannabis with consistent high drug yields from Hortapharm and by the late 1990s was growing and harvesting a crop of 5000 plants. To avoid the variable absorption of ingested cannabis, the firm decided to produce a spray to be applied under the tongue, where it would be quickly absorbed into the bloodstream. And so Sativex was born.

Notcutt agreed to carry out a clinical trial. But despite increasing public acceptance of the idea of using cannabis medicinally, he found it hard to get the study approved by his hospital.

It took about a year to get the go-ahead for a small three-month study in people, some with MS, for whom existing treatments were ineffective against chronic pain. The results, published last year [2004], showed that Sativex provided significant pain relief for 28 of the 34 patients in the study. GW began larger trials on people with MS or chronic pain, as well as pilot studies in people with cancer.

Finding a Market for Sativex

At this point GW began looking for a pharmaceutical company with the muscle and money to help market Sativex. Rumours circulating at the end of 2002 suggested that Guy was in talks with a major-league company, perhaps GlaxoSmith-Kline or AstraZeneca. Guy won't say, because before the deal was done, the firm got cold feet. They were spooked by the "c-word", Guy says. Cannabis was too controversial for the American board members. GW had to find another partner, and in May 2004 it finally struck a deal with the German-based multinational Bayer.

In the meantime, the larger clinical trials were starting to yield positive results. GW has applied for a licence from the Medicines and Healthcare Products Regulatory Agency (MHRA) to sell the drug in the UK. The MHRA has asked for a "confirmatory study," to prove that the reduction in muscle spasticity seen with Sativex brings meaningful benefits to patients. GW says this will take several months.

But it is in Canada, where patients can legally use cannabis for medicinal purposes, that Sativex is closest to being licensed. The preparation was given preliminary approval in December [2004], and GW and the Canadian regulatory agency are now thrashing out exact terms for a licence to allow Sativex to be sold as a prescription drug. Assuming they reach agreement, Sativex could reach pharmacies within a couple of months. GW says it will be applying for licences in "other Commonwealth countries," probably Australia and New Zealand.

Other Cannabis-Based Drugs in the Works

It may not be long before Sativex is joined by other cannabis preparations. A non-profit group, the Institute for Clinical Research in Berlin, Germany, is developing oral cannabis capsules, called Cannador. In November 2003 a study in 630 MS [multiple sclerosis] patients produced equivocal results. While the formal scoring system for measuring muscle spasticity indicated that Cannador performed no better than a placebo, the patients themselves felt it helped. Martin Schnelle, who conducted the trial, says that there are widely acknowledged problems with the formal scoring system used. "There are medicines that are already licensed for treating spasticity that have failed on this scale," he says. The group is planning a further study this year in which the patients' reports will be the main measure by which the drug's effectiveness is judged.

In the US, the NIDA has become more open to research on the benefits of cannabis, and Abrams is studying its ability to ease pain due to nerve damage in HIV, and nausea and vomiting after cancer chemotherapy. He is investigating a device called the Volcano, which heats cannabis to the point of vaporisation without burning it, which he says is less harmful than smoking it in a joint because it releases fewer carcinogens. While Abrams welcomes products like Sativex, he suggests that some people will always prefer marijuana to a commercial preparation—not least because they can grow it themselves.

But however cultural attitudes to street or home-grown cannabis change, its availability in standardised, licensed preparations such as Sativex and perhaps Cannador will be the key to its wider medical use. GW is planning studies of its possible benefits for people with a range of conditions from Crohn's disease to rheumatoid arthritis and heroin addiction. If positive, Canada's decision will signal a big change in the status of cannabis, says Philip Robson, the firm's medical director. "It's the dawning of a new clinical research era."

Pharmaceutical Versions of Marijuana Offer Promise

Gary Greenberg

Gary Greenberg extensively surveyed the recent progress that has been made in developing medical alternatives to smoked marijuana for patients who suffer from nausea, chronic pain, AIDS, cancer, and multiple sclerosis. In the following article, Greenberg recounts how a privately owned British drug company, GW Pharmaceuticals, successfully petitioned the British government to mass-produce high-grade marijuana and conduct clinical trials on a marijuana-derived mouth spray called Sativex. The drug has been approved for use in the UK and Canada and is poised to undergo rigorous government testing in the United States. Greenberg reports that entrepreneurs in the United States are fearful that GW could eventually land a billion-dollar monopoly on pharmaceutical marijuana. Organizations such as the Multidisciplinary Association for Psychedelic Studies (MAPS) have been trying for years to secure federal government approval to grow and test their own version of medical marijuana, a form that would introduce the drug through a vaporization process. Either way, Greenberg argues, if a form of medical marijuana is approved in the United States, the political consequences would be enormous: Prohibitionists will be forced to acknowledge that marijuana does have medicinal properties after all and decriminalization advocates will lose a wedge issue if other methods of ingesting marijuana are deemed as effective or superior to smoking it.

If it weren't for the little photo gallery on the wall, the office where Dr. William Notcutt's research assistants keep track of their patients would be just like any other cubicle at the

Gary Greenberg, "Respectable Reefer," *Mother Jones*, November–December 2005. Copyright 2005 Foundation for National Progress. Reproduced by permission.

James Paget Medical Center in England. As phones ring and stretchers wheel by and these three women go about their business, the snapshots—Cheryl Phillips, one of Notcutt's staffers, gently holding an emerald green bud of marijuana; a group of people in lab coats smiling for the camera, sinsemilla towering over their heads; a hangar-sized greenhouse stuffed to the gills with lush pot plants—are about the only evidence that this hospital in East Anglia is at the epicenter of one of the most extensive medical marijuana research projects in the world. In part, that's because there's no actual pot here; by the time it gets to Paget, GW Pharmaceuticals, the British startup that owns the greenhouses, has turned the plants into Sativex, a pure extract of pot that comes in a pharmacy-friendly bottle and is designed to be sprayed into the mouth. And in part it's because the frivolity is carefully confined to the photos, taken against company policy during a field trip to the secure, un-disclosed location where GW grows its weed. After five years, Phillips and her colleagues have grown used to having can-nabis—as the British call marijuana—in their workaday lives. Not only that, but their boss has been on a bit of a campaign to keep things sober. "To get to the perception that this is a medicine," Notcutt says, "we've had to move away from the funnies that relate to the pot world. So no pot jokes."

Over a beer at the end of his day, this rumpled, 59-year-old anesthesiologist and contract researcher for GW is posi-tively ebullient about the news that just today [April 19, 2005] the Canadian government approved Sativex, a success he thinks is likely to be repeated soon in England and eventually in the United States. He'll gladly tell you how important ear-nestness has been in getting GW to this point, how Sativex owes its success not only to the rigorous science of its success-ful clinical trials but also to painstaking attention to matters of perception.

A Legitimate Medicine

Take the spray concept. There are sound medical reasons for spraying cannabis under the tongue rather than smoking or eating it. The mucosa of the mouth will absorb the drug faster than the digestive system, indeed almost as fast as the lungs, but without irritating the respiratory system. And Sativex can be precisely metered—a single one-tenth milliliter spray contains 2.7 milligrams of tetrahydrocannabinol (THC), pot's main psychoactive chemical; 2.5 milligrams of cannabidiol, which doctors think reduces anxiety and muscle tension; and all of pot's active ingredients known as cannabinoids—so that it can be accurately studied. But it also has "the advantage of looking like a medicine to the outside world," Notcutt says. "It has been served up like a medicine, prepared like a medicine, researched like a medicine. It looks like a medicine, and it's prescribed like a medicine." Taking pot out of joints scored on the street and putting it into bottles found on pharmacy shelves shows that "we're not just being silly about the herb, even though in the end that's exactly what it is. It's as if you just squeezed the plant," he says, wringing an imaginary stalk in his hands.

Notcutt began trying to medicalize cannabis more than a decade ago, and has been working with GW and its founder and executive chairman, Geoffrey Guy, since the company's inception in 1998. He credits Guy (who wouldn't be interviewed for this article) with hitting upon the spray, just one of the measures he's taken to distance Sativex from its unsavory origins. Guy has styled GW, which he started solely to develop cannabis medicines, as just another drug company seeking to develop just another drug. He raised money in the usual ways—first from private investors, then with a 2001 stock offering that garnered $48 million, and finally, in 2003, with an estimated $65 million licensing deal with German pharmaceutical giant Bayer—and used it to purchase the rights to pot varieties that a Dutch company had spent millions of dollars and more than a decade developing for their medicinal properties. Guy presents himself as neutral in the drug wars and gained the support of the British government by offering to institute extraordinary security measures at his grow facility to prevent "diversion." The British government, in turn, gave him permission to grow his pot and test it on human subjects and so exempted GW from an international treaty forbidding private production of outlawed drugs. Guy developed a way to blend the plants (a process he has likened to making blended burgundies) into precise mixtures whose chemical profiles can be standardized (which regulators like), patented (which investors like; cannabis itself can't be patented), and then described in company press releases as "a novel prescription pharmaceutical product derived from components of the cannabis plant."

Having successfully distilled pot's reputation as a medicine from its reputation as a way to get high, Notcutt says, "the powers that be at GW worked hard to maintain this myth. We start in that comfort area, we don't talk about anything outside this comfort area." This hard work has no doubt paid off in Canada and England, reassuring regulators that, as Notcutt put it, "we're talking about a serious medical subject here." The real audience for all this mythmaking, however, isn't Britain or Canada, which will ultimately account for only a small percentage of the cannabinoid drug market, estimated to be almost $1 billion a year. It's the United States, where, Notcutt says, things are different. "Marijuanaphobia is much greater on your side of the pond," he told me. "We've never had the reefer madness."

Dispelling Marijuana Phobia in the United States

Since pot was prohibited in 1937, there's been a virtual epidemic of this malady in the U.S., and GW's posturing seems designed to exploit its latest manifestation: the strange politics of the pitched battle over medical marijuana. The federal government lists cannabis in all its forms on Schedule I of the Controlled Substances Act, a designation reserved for drugs that it says are unsafe and have no known medical use. But medical marijuana activists, drawing on a growing body of evidence indicating that cannabis is a safe and effective medicine, especially for nausea and spasmodic pain, have clamored for its legalization for medical purposes. And they've gained support among the general public. Eleven states have passed medical marijuana laws; no state ballot initiative put before voters has ever failed to pass.

Some of the resulting controversy breaks down along predictable lines—chronically ill people accusing the government of withholding treatment while the government denounces medical marijuana as a "cruel hoax;" legalization advocates hoping to use medical marijuana as a wedge issue while drug warriors warn that it's a Trojan horse. But recently new political fissures have opened up. In *Gonzales v. Raich*, a case brought to the Supreme Court after the feds busted a medical marijuana patient over the objections of California sheriffs, the Court recently determined that this was "a valid exercise of federal power," but Justice John Paul Stevens' majority opinion was rife with regret about "the troubling facts of the case." Alabama, Louisiana, and Mississippi, three states not exactly known for their liberal traditions, filed briefs in support of the patients, urging the justices to allow states to exercise their function as "laboratories for experimentation." And three justices—including Clarence Thomas and William Rehnquist—dissented on the grounds that medical marijuana should be an issue for individual states to decide, thus placing two of America's most prominent conservatives on the same side of the issue as George Soros [a global financier and philanthropist] and Barney Frank [Democratic senator from Massachusetts], another ideological divide gone up in smoke.

The significance of the medical marijuana skirmish goes well beyond its fractured politics or its implications for federalism. Even as the government ratchets up prohibition—it currently spends $4 billion a year just arresting and prosecuting people for marijuana-related crimes—evidence of cannabis' safety and efficacy accumulates and the cornerstone of marijuana prohibition weakens. With stakes this high, it's no wonder that judges and politicians, and maybe the rest of us, are dazed and confused about medical marijuana. And it's also no wonder that GW is already garnering notice in the U.S. or that it has managed to attract prominent drug warriors, including the government's leading anti-medical-marijuana spokeswoman, to its cause. Sativex, the pot that dares not speak its name, may be exactly what the doctor ordered: a way for drug warriors to squeeze between the rock of prohibition and the hard place of patients clamoring for medicine. With a prescription version of cannabis available in pharmacies, the feds could regain their moral authority to raid your backyard garden, disrupt the delicate alliances the medical marijuana movement has spawned, and deprive legalizers of what may be their most powerful wedge issue. GW may end up, that is, with a shareholder's dream: a monopoly welcomed by policymakers and enforced by the police, leaving medical marijuana activists to wish they'd been more careful about what they'd asked for.

A Pioneer in American Medical Marijuana Research

England isn't the only place where clinical trials of cannabis are being conducted. In fact, on ward 5-B of San Francisco General Hospital—once the site of the world's first dedicated AIDS unit—there are two rooms with oversize exhaust fans where patients can smoke marijuana in the name of science. Sometimes the staff has to put towels under the doors to prevent the smoke and smell from permeating the hallway. . . .

[Dr. Donald] Abrams, a professor of medicine at the University of California–San Francisco who was one of the first people to suggest that a virus causes AIDS, knows all about working with stoned people. He's one of the few American scientists allowed to study pot in human subjects. Since 1992, he's been trying to bring some scientific law and order to the medical marijuana frontier, where patients take pot for complaints ranging from chemotherapy-related nausea to menstrual cramps and where, in California anyway, dispensaries function without much regulation. But progress has been slow, in part because it has been difficult to fill his studies: He recently had to close down a cancer pain trial for lack of subjects, and patients don't always complete the studies. Half the subjects in the neuropathy study get pot that has been denuded of THC. "Nobody gets fooled for long," says Abrams, and he worries that David [an AIDS-related-pain patient] may go the way of a recent subject who said, "I don't want to be here for a week smoking a placebo when I can get real pot out on the street," and bailed.

Government Approval Proves Difficult to Secure

But at least [Abrams is] fretting about recruiting and retaining patients rather than whether he's going to be allowed to do the research in the first place. It took five years to get his first trial—initially a study to determine whether marijuana would help people with AIDS-wasting syndrome—under way. He had his FDA approval within a year, but acquiring the pot to actually run the study proved nearly impossible. He couldn't just buy it on the street or grow it in his backyard like everyone else. He needed a drug that the FDA would accept as pure and that was legally obtained. So he applied for a license from the Drug Enforcement Agency to import research-grade weed (from the same Dutch company that supplies GW). The DEA stonewalled him, as did the National Institutes on Drug Abuse, the nation's only legal supplier, when he asked for some of the pot grown for NIDA at the University of Mississippi. NIDA eventually denied his request, on the grounds that the FDA-approved study was not "scientific" enough. Abrams persisted, however, and NIDA finally relented in 1997, after Abrams overhauled his study so as to investigate marijuana's potential harms to people taking protease inhibitors—a strategy he says he adopted after Alan Leshner, then NIDA's director, reminded him that "we're the National Institutes on Drug Abuse, not the National Institutes for Drug Abuse." (Leshner declined to comment.)

Abrams says he can now get NIDA pot when he needs it. But the six studies he has run have enrolled only 161 people and are still in the preliminary stages of proving pot's efficacy and safety. Meanwhile, GW has tested Sativex on more than 1,000 subjects, and is well into the late stages of the kind of clinical testing required by the FDA. Abrams won't comment directly on Sativex. ("I'm just not a political person," he says repeatedly.) Nor will he speculate about the commercial implications of his research, about how, or even whether, pot ought to be brought to market (or back to market; Abrams points out that cannabis was used medically for thousands of years prior to its prohibition), or about GW's lead in the race to restore cannabis to legitimacy.

The Drive to Research a Plant-Based Care

Rick Doblin, on the other hand, will. Doblin heads the Multidisciplinary Association for Psychedelic Studies [MAPS], a nonprofit organization that first applied to develop marijuana as a treatment for AIDS wasting (Abrams' first study was originally intended for MAPS), and he has been trying unsuccessfully to launch medical marijuana research for nearly 15 years. MAPS, like GW, wants to develop cannabis as a pharmaceutical drug, but, as Doblin puts it, "in the least refined, least expensive way possible—as plant material that people can get in pharmacies or as plants or seeds that they can grow and process themselves." Doblin envisions patients choosing among a number of methods of taking the drug, but he's especially keen on vaporizing, which he thinks may answer concerns about smoking. But he hasn't been able to investigate this hunch. "We can get the FDA to work with us, but we can't get pot from NIDA," says Doblin. "We've been waiting for two years just for a decision on whether they'll sell us 10 grams for our vaporizer study." Doblin thinks that NIDA is "scared of the research. If we prove that it's not true that pot pushes people into schizophrenia or causes lung cancer, if it's not doing the things the government says are the reasons it's bad, then we undercut their credibility."

But even if NIDA were a reliable supplier, Doblin says, "we don't want their weed." NIDA's brown, stems-and-seeds-laden, low-potency pot—what's known on the streets as "schwag"—cannot stack up against the dense green, aromatic, and powerful sinsemilla favored by most medical marijuana patients (and grown by GW). Doblin asked the University of Mississippi to grow the good stuff for him, but they refused, so he approached a botanist at the University of Massachusetts, who applied to the DEA to grow research-grade pot in a 200-square-foot room in the basement of a building in Amherst. This started a whole new kind of collegiate rivalry, the Rebels squaring off against the Minutemen over the quality of their pot. In a letter to the DEA, Mississippi's botanist—after pointing out that no one had ever officially complained about the "adequacy" of their product—trumpeted recently acquired "custom-manufactured deseeding equipment" and a new stock of seeds that had allowed Ole Miss to amass more than 50,000 joints' worth of a "special batch" of high-potency, smooth-smoking weed. Three and a half years after UMass kicked off the battle—and only after a judge ordered the feds to make their decision—the Rebels prevailed, its monopoly preserved when the DEA denied UMass the license necessary to grow pot legally.

MAPS is appealing the decision through the DEA's administrative law court. But while the bureaucratic process crawls along, the organization's attempt to bring pharmaceutical-grade, inexpensive pot to patients is at a standstill. "We can way outcompete GW in a legal market," Doblin says. (In Canada, a month's supply of Sativex will cost patients using nine sprays a day about $500, comparable to other multiple sclerosis drugs and about the same as a month's supply of pot bought at California medical marijuana clubs.) "But if you're going to invest millions of dollars in drug development," he continues, "you have to have an uninterrupted supply. We don't even have a pilot study. We're nowhere." As a result, GW, with its government-sanctioned greenhouses yielding 60 tons of high-quality pot every year, is lightyears ahead of its nearest American competitor and, according to Doblin, it has drug warriors to thank for its lead. "They're going to let this whole market go to the Brits."

Paving the Way for Sativex in the United States

At least one person in the States would like to [gain access to the Sativex spray]. Julie Falco, a Chicagoan who has had MS for half of her 40 years, bakes an ounce of pot into a pan of brownies ("I like a little chocolate with my cannabis," she says) every 10 days or so and eats a small square every morning for pain and spasticity. She sees Sativex as "another option in the arsenal," one that can provide quicker relief than eating pot and can be used in public. But getting Sativex from Canada is not as easy as hopping on a bus and buying Prilosec. Even if she could get a prescription, U.S. Customs and Border Protection would, according to a spokesman, seize and destroy Sativex on the grounds that cannabis is illegal in this country. So Falco has applied to the FDA for permission to obtain Sativex under the Compassionate Use program, which allows patients for whom there is no other treatment to obtain drugs still considered experimental by the U.S. government. (More than 40 medical marijuana patients once got pot directly from the government under this program, but in 1992 the FDA stopped considering Compassionate Use applications for the plant.)

Even if Falco is successful, most patients will have to wait for Sativex to run the FDA's gauntlet—notoriously difficult and unpredictable even for drugs without political baggage. But there is precedent for FDA approval of cannabinoids. In 1985, the agency approved Marinol, a synthetic form of THC, as a treatment for AIDS-related wasting and chemotherapy-induced nausea, but it has proved unpopular with patients, who complain that the drug takes too long to work, which makes the dosage hard to adjust, and that it is ineffective. (Some scientists believe that pot's medicinal effects depend on the interaction among all its chemicals, not just on THC.) Drug policymakers had hoped Marinol would be "a godsend," according to Mark Kleiman, director of the Drug Policy Analysis Program at UCLA's School of Public Affairs. "It wasn't any fun and made the user feel bad," Kleiman says, "so it could be approved without any fear that it would penetrate the recreational market, and then used as a club with which to beat back the advocates of whole cannabis as a medicine." Kleiman thinks that Sativex might succeed where Marinol failed, not only because evidence from GW's clinical trials might convince regulators that it works, but also because GW is poised to "persuade the drug warriors that getting Sativex approved fast is the best way to block the medical marijuana movement."

The Political Consequences of Approving Sativex

But this kind of maneuvering could have unintended consequences. "The approval of Sativex will show that the drug warriors have been lying all along about medical marijuana," says Rob Kampia, head of the Marijuana Policy Project, an organization that has spearheaded several state ballot initiatives.

It will also, Kampia thinks, vastly complicate law enforcement efforts. "If Sativex is approved in the U.S., and a patient is arrested for whole marijuana and they go to court, they're now going to be able to say, 'Hey, we know that liquid marijuana has medical value as declared by the FDA, therefore I shouldn't go to prison for having nonliquid marijuana.'"

UCLA's Kleiman points out other complications for drug warriors: "If the word gets out that in fact it can be used to get high, then there might be a substantial demand for it among those who want to get stoned while remaining within the law, especially since it could be prescribed for relatively nonspecific indications such as pain and anxiety. And the one thing this is going to do for sure," he adds, "is wreck the drug-testing industry."

GW refuses to comment on these possibilities, calling drug policy "a matter for lawyers and governments." But drug-war politics matter to the company, if for no other reason than that prohibition would make Sativex the only legal cannabis in the marketplace. . . . Indeed without prohibition, GW might not have a market, which may be why, in addition to its larger population, the United States holds more appeal to the company than Canada and Europe, with their relatively lax laws.

A couple of GW hires indicate that the company is not nearly so apolitical as it claims: John Pastuovic, a campaign spokesman for George W. Bush in 2000 who was part of an effort to derail medical marijuana legislation in Illinois earlier this year, and Andrea Barthwell, who, as a deputy drug czar from 2002 to 2004, led the campaign to brand medical marijuana as a hoax. Both can be expected to enforce message discipline. As soon as I told him I was writing about medical marijuana, Pastuovic interrupted. "Sativex is not medical marijuana," he said. "What you have out [in California], that's medical marijuana. Sativex is medicine." For her part, Barthwell has refused to publicly comment about her turnaround, except to say to the *Los Angeles Times* that "comparing crude marijuana to Sativex is like comparing a raging forest fire to the fire in your home's furnace. While both provide heat, one is out of control."

Kampia says [that] "Sativex fits the niche that the drug warriors have created." And they seem to agree. "It is entirely possible that there are elements of the cannabis plant that have medicinal value," says Tom Riley, spokesman for the drug czar's office, echoing an Institute of Medicine report that his office commissioned in 1999. "If such elements were developed into safe, effective medicines, they could theoretically be prescribed and distributed like all the other drugs that have dependency-producing side effects."

Sativex also fits a niche that Kampia's movement has created, if inadvertently, by seeking to legitimize pot as a medicine even as it remains otherwise illegal. In a society that relies on a profit-driven, science-based industry to supply drugs and on government regulators to approve them, a raw herb that grows like a weed and has been vilified for nearly 70 years is a tough sell as a medicine. A patented liquid that you can pick up at Walgreens along with your Prozac, on the other hand, may be precisely the formula for bringing cannabis in out of the cold, especially if it has a carefully crafted reputation as something other than pot.

It is, of course, way too early to tell, but within two days of the Canadian approval, U.S. newspapers were already reporting that Sativex consisted of a "type of cannabinoids that have been isolated and purified [to] work specifically at the targeted pain receptors," and that the drug "does not intoxicate users." That, according to Willy Notcutt, "is a load of bollocks. But why," he asked me, "correct such misapprehensions at the current time?"

State and Federal Governments Differ on Medical Marijuana Use

Susan Okie

In the following article Susan Okie details the circumstances surrounding the 2005 Supreme Court case known as Gonzales v. Raich. *This legal battle pitted the U.S. federal government, intent on the total prohibition of marijuana use, against Angel McClary Raich, a California woman who takes the drug to relieve symptoms associated with an undiagnosed wasting syndrome. In a 6–3 ruling against Raich, the Supreme Court maintained that under the Controlled Substances Act of 1970 the federal government has the right to police the interstate trade in illegal drugs. Okie observes that the court's decision touched off a national controversy involving the constitutional protection of personal and state rights because it affirmed that patients who use marijuana in states where its consumption for medical purposes is legal are still subject to arrest and prosecution by federal authorities. Okie acknowledges that despite the Supreme Court ruling, marijuana reform leaders and civil rights activists will continue to fight the federal government in the court system on the issue of medical marijuana.*

Angel McClary Raich, a California woman at the center of the recent Supreme Court case on medical marijuana, hasn't changed her treatment regimen since the Court ruled in June that patients who take the drug in states where its medicinal use is legal are not shielded from federal prosecution. A thin woman with long, dark hair and an intense gaze, Raich takes marijuana, or cannabis as she prefers to call it, about ev-

Susan Okie, "Medical Marijuana and the Supreme Court," *New England Journal of Medicine*, vol. 353, August 15, 2005, pp. 648–651. © 2005 Massachusetts Medical Society. All rights reserved. Reproduced by permission.

ery two waking hours—by smoking it, by inhaling it as a vapor, by eating it in foods, or by applying it topically as a balm. She says that it relieves her chronic pain and boosts her appetite, preventing her from becoming emaciated because of a mysterious wasting syndrome. Raich and her doctor maintain that without access to the eight or nine pounds of privately grown cannabis that she consumes each year, she would die.

The cannabis is placed in the chamber and heated to a temperature below that required for combustion. The balloon fills with vapor that contains the active ingredients without the tar or particulates thought to be responsible for most of the drug's adverse effects on the respiratory tract. The patient inhales the vapor from the balloon.

Although Raich has embraced a public role advocating the medicinal use of marijuana, she says that her health suffered during the hectic days following the announcement of the Court's decision, when a whirlwind schedule of press conferences and congressional meetings in Washington prevented her from medicating herself with cannabis as regularly as she needed to. "My body was shutting down on me," she said in an interview from her Oakland home last month. "I'm scared of my health failing. I'm scared of the federal government coming in and doing more harm. [Recently,] the city of Oakland warned there were going to be some raids" on marijuana dispensaries. "We're all just waiting. Sitting on the frontline is extremely stressful."

In the Supreme Court case *Gonzales v. Raich*, the justices ruled 6 to 3 that the federal government has the power to arrest and prosecute patients and their suppliers even if the marijuana use is permitted under state law, because of its authority under the federal Controlled Substances Act to regulate interstate commerce in illegal drugs. In practical terms, it is not yet clear what effect the Court's decision will have on patients. An estimated 115,000 people have obtained recommendations for marijuana from doctors in the 10 states that have legalized the cultivation, possession, and use of mari-juana for medicinal purposes. Besides California, those states are Alaska, Colorado, Hawaii, Maine, Montana, Nevada, Oregon, Vermont, and Washington. (Three weeks after the decision was announced, Rhode Island's legislature passed a similar law and soon afterward overrode a veto by the state's governor.)

Immediately after the news of the high court's ruling, attorneys general in the states that have approved the use of medical marijuana emphasized that the practice remained legal under their state laws, and a telephone survey of a random national sample of registered voters, commissioned by the Washington-based Marijuana Policy Project, indicated that 68 percent of respondents opposed federal prosecution of patients who use marijuana for medical reasons. Nationally, most marijuana arrests are made by state and local law-enforcement agencies, with federal arrests accounting for only about 1 percent of cases. However, soon after the decision was announced, federal agents raided 3 of San Francisco's more than 40 medical marijuana dispensaries. Nineteen people were charged with running an international drug ring; they allegedly were using the dispensaries as a front for trafficking in marijuana and in the illegal amphetamine "ecstasy."

In California, the raids were widely viewed as a signal that federal drug-enforcement agents intended to crack down on abuse of the state's medical marijuana program. California has an estimated 100,000 medical marijuana users. Its 1996 law grants doctors much greater latitude in recommending the drug than do similar laws in other states, and the U.S. District Court for the Northern District of California ruled in 2000 that doctors who prescribe marijuana are protected from federal prosecution under the First Amendment, provided that they do not help their patients obtain the drug. In San Francisco, some journalists or investigators who posed as patients have reported that they had little difficulty obtaining a recommendation for medical marijuana, which allows the holder to purchase the drug from a dispensary. "We're empathetic to the sick," the Drug Enforcement Administration's Javier Pena told reporters after the raids, "but we can't disregard the federal law."[1]

Even before the Supreme Court decision, many Californians had been calling for stricter state regulation of medical marijuana. Some cities have banned marijuana dispensaries, and many counties and cities—including San Francisco—have imposed moratoriums on the opening of new ones. Some local jurisdictions register and issue identification cards to patients who use marijuana for medical reasons, and state officials have been working on a voluntary statewide registration program. However, the officials recently put the program on hold, citing concern that the issuance of identification cards to patients might put state health officials at risk of prosecution for aiding a federal crime and that federal drug-enforcement agents might seek state records in order to identify medical marijuana users. Registration of patients and the issuance of identification cards by the state are required in seven other states that have legalized the medical use of marijuana; patients can show the card as a defense against arrest by local or state police for possession of the drug. Maine and Washington do not issue identification cards to patients.

Conditions for which marijuana is commonly recommended include nausea caused by cancer chemotherapy; anorexia or wasting due to cancer, AIDS, or other diseases; chronic pain; spasticity caused by multiple sclerosis or other neurologic disorders; and glaucoma. Frank Lucido, a Berkeley family practitioner who is Raich's doctor, said that so far, the Court ruling appears to have had little effect on his patients who use medical marijuana. About 30 percent of Lucido's practice consists of evaluating patients who want a recommendation for the drug. He said in an interview that he will not issue such a recommendation unless a patient has a primary care physician and has a condition serious enough to require follow-up at least annually. About 80 percent of his patients who use medical cannabis have chronic pain; a smaller number take the drug for muscle spasms, mood disorders, migraine, AIDS, or cancer. "My patients probably average in their 30s," Lucido said. "I have had probably five patients who are under 18. These are people with serious illnesses, where parents were very clear that this would be a good medication for them."

Peter A. Rasmussen, an oncologist in Salem, Oregon, said he discusses the option of trying marijuana with about 1 in 10 patients in his practice. "It's not my first choice for any symptom," he said in an interview. "I only talk about it with people if my first-line treatment doesn't work." Rasmussen said marijuana has helped stimulate appetite or reduce nausea in a number of his patients with cancer, but others have been distressed by its psychological effects. Some express interest in trying marijuana but have difficulty getting the drug. "Most of my patients who use it, I think, just buy the drug illegally," he said. "But a lot of my patients, they're older, they don't know any kids, they don't hang out on the street. They just don't know how to get it."

Clinical research on marijuana has been hampered by the fact that the plant, which contains dozens of active substances, is an illegal drug classified as having no legitimate medical use. Researchers wishing to do clinical studies must first get government permission and obtain a supply of the drug from the National Institute on Drug Abuse. In a report published in 1999, an expert committee of the Institute of Medicine expressed concern about the adverse health effects of smoking marijuana, particularly on the respiratory tract. The report called for expanded research on marijuana's active components, known as cannabinoids, including studies to explore the chemicals' potential therapeutic effects and to develop safe, reliable, rapid-onset delivery systems. It also recommended short-term clinical trials of marijuana "in patients with conditions for which there is reasonable expectation of efficacy."[2]

There has been some progress toward those goals. The Center for Medicinal Cannabis Research (CMCR), a three-year research initiative established in 1999 by the California state legislature, has funded several placebo-controlled clinical trials of smoked marijuana to treat neuropathic pain, pain from other causes, and spasticity in multiple sclerosis, and the results are likely to be available soon. The National Institute on Drug Abuse provided both the active marijuana and the "placebo," a smokable version of the drug from which dronabinol (Delta 9-tetrahydrocannabinol, or THC) and certain other active constituents had been removed. "It's like decaf coffee or nicotine-free cigarettes, and it tastes the same [as marijuana]," said Igor Grant, a professor of psychiatry at the University of California, San Diego, and director of the CMCR. He said additional studies of the whole plant, as well as its individual components, are still needed. "It's still the case that we don't know which components of botanical marijuana have beneficial effects, if any," he said.

In an open-label trial, oncologist Donald I. Abrams of the University of California, San Francisco, found evidence of marijuana's effectiveness in the treatment of neuropathic pain among HIV-infected patients and has just finished a placebo-controlled trial that he intends to publish soon. Abrams has also shown that cannabinoids that are smoked or taken orally do not adversely affect drug treatment of HIV[3], and he is completing a study that compares blood levels of cannabinoids among volunteers who inhaled vaporized marijuana with similar levels among volunteers who smoked the drug. Vaporizers heat the drug to a temperature below that required for combustion, producing vapor that contains the active ingredients without the tar or particulates thought to be responsible for most of the drug's adverse effects on the respiratory tract.

Meanwhile, a new marijuana-derived drug is on the Canadian market and may soon be considered for approval by the Food and Drug Administration. Sativex, a liquid cannabis extract that is sprayed under the tongue, was approved in Canada in June for the treatment of neuropathic pain in multiple sclerosis. Its principal active ingredients are dronabinol and cannabidiol, which are believed to be the primary active components of marijuana. The drug's manufacturer, GW Pharmaceuticals of Britain, is also testing it for cancer pain, rheumatoid arthritis, postoperative pain, and other indications. Marinol, a synthetic version of dronabinol supplied in capsules, is approved in the United States for chemotherapy-associated nausea and for anorexia and wasting among patients with AIDS.

On the day the Supreme Court ruling was announced, John Walters, President George W. Bush's "drug czar," issued a statement declaring, "Today's decision marks the end of medical marijuana as a political issue.... We have a responsibility as a civilized society to ensure that the medicine Americans receive from their doctors is effective, safe, and free from the pro-drug politics that are being promoted in America under the guise of medicine." Nine days later, the House of Representatives, for the third year in a row, defeated a measure that would have prevented the Justice Department from spending money to prosecute medical marijuana cases under federal law.

Nevertheless, marijuana advocates insist that the long-running battle between federal and state governments over the medicinal use of marijuana is far from over. Activists next plan to focus on getting more states to pass laws legalizing medical marijuana, according to Steve Fox, former director of government relations for the Marijuana Policy Project.

It is surprising that the Supreme Court decision does not necessarily spell the end even of Angel Raich's legal case. Raich and another California patient, Diane Monson, who initially sued to prevent the Justice Department from prosecuting them or their suppliers, won a favorable ruling in 2003 from California's Court of Appeals for the Ninth Circuit. The Supreme Court's reversal now sends their case back to that court. Raich said that she, Monson, and their attorneys will ask the appeals court judges to consider other legal arguments, such as whether prosecuting patients who use marijuana to relieve pain violates their right to due process of law. "Previous decisions have established that there is a fundamental right to preserve one's life and avoid needless pain and suffering," explained Boston University's Randy Barnett, a constitutional lawyer who argued the women's case before the Supreme Court. "Federal restriction on accessibility to medical cannabis is an infringement" on that right, he said.

Raich vowed to continue her personal battle. "I'm stubborn as heck, so I don't plan to give it up that easily. I plan to fight until I can't fight anymore," she said.

Notes

1. Finz, S. 19, "Named in Medicinal Pot Indictment," *San Francisco Chronicle*, June 24, 2005: B4.
2. Joy, J.E., Watson S.J., Benson J.A., eds., *Marijuana and Medicine: Assessing the Science Base*. Washington, DC.: National Academy Press, 1999.
3. Abrams, D.I., Hilton, J.F., Leiser, R.J., et al, "Short-Term Effects of Cannabinoids in Patients with HIV-1 Infection: A Randomized, Placebo-Controlled Clinical Trial," Ann Intern Med 2003, 139, 258–266.

CHAPTER 3

The Fight to Legalize Marijuana

Popular Support Has Increased for Marijuana Legalization

Ethan A. Nadelmann

Ethan A. Nadelmann is the founder and executive director of the Drug Policy Alliance, an organization dedicated to reforming U.S. drug policies through the application of science, compassion, and health and human rights. He documents the growing support among Americans for the decriminalization of marijuana for recreational and medicinal use. The enforcement of current marijuana laws, Nadelmann argues, is too severe and costly given that some 87 percent of arrests are made merely for possession of small amounts of the drug. He also calls attention to the medical marijuana debate, pointing out that while the federal government refuses to permit the drug's use for medical purposes, every state ballot initiative relating to medical marijuana has been approved by voters. In fact, Nadelmann sees the medical marijuana movement as the key to ending the drug's prohibition in the United States.

Never before have so many Americans supported decriminalizing and even legalizing marijuana. Seventy-two percent say that for simple marijuana possession, people should not be incarcerated but fined: the generally accepted definition of "decriminalization." Even more Americans support making marijuana legal for medical purposes. Support for broader legalization ranges between 25 and 42 percent, depending on how one asks the question. Two of every five Americans—

according to a 2003 Zogby poll—say "the government should treat marijuana more or less the same way it treats alcohol: It should regulate it, control it, tax it, and only make it illegal for children."

Close to 100 million Americans—including more than half of those between the ages of 18 and 50—have tried marijuana at least once. Military and police recruiters often have no choice but to ignore past marijuana use by job seekers. The public apparently feels the same way about presidential and other political candidates. Al Gore, Bill Bradley, and John Kerry all say they smoked pot in days past. So did Bill Clinton, with his notorious caveat. George W. Bush won't deny he did. And ever more political, business, religious, intellectual, and other leaders plead guilty as well.

The debate over ending marijuana prohibition simmers just below the surface of mainstream politics, crossing ideological and partisan boundaries. Marijuana is no longer the symbol of Sixties rebellion and Seventies permissiveness, and it's not just liberals and libertarians who say it should be legal, as William F. Buckley Jr. has demonstrated better than anyone. As director of the country's leading drug-policy-reform organization, I've had countless conversations with police and prosecutors, judges and politicians, and hundreds of others who quietly agree that the criminalization of marijuana is costly, foolish, and destructive. What's most needed now is principled conservative leadership. Buckley has led the way, and New Mexico's former governor, Gary Johnson, spoke out courageously while in office. How about others?

A Systemic Overreaction

Marijuana prohibition is unique among American criminal laws. No other law is both enforced so widely and harshly and yet deemed unnecessary by such a substantial portion of the populace.

Police make about 700,000 arrests per year for marijuana offenses. That's almost the same number as are arrested each year for cocaine, heroin, methamphetamine, Ecstasy, and all other illicit drugs combined. Roughly 600,000, or 87 percent, of marijuana arrests are for nothing more than possession of small amounts. Millions of Americans have never been arrested or convicted of any criminal offense except this. Enforcing marijuana laws costs an estimated $10–15 billion in direct costs alone.

Punishments range widely across the country, from modest fines to a few days in jail to many years in prison. Prosecutors often contend that no one goes to prison for simple possession—but tens, perhaps hundreds, of thousands of people on probation and parole are locked up each year because their urine tested positive for marijuana or because they were picked up in possession of a joint. Alabama currently locks up people convicted three times of marijuana *possession* for 15 years to life. There are probably—no firm estimates exist—100,000 Americans behind bars tonight for one marijuana offense or another. And even for those who don't lose their freedom, simply being arrested can be traumatic and costly. A parent's marijuana use can be the basis for taking away her children and putting them in foster care. Foreign-born residents of the U.S. can be deported for a marijuana offense no matter how long they have lived in this country, no matter if their children are U.S. citizens, and no matter how long they have been legally employed. More than half the states revoke or suspend driver's licenses of people arrested for marijuana possession even though they were not driving at the time of arrest. The federal Higher Education Act prohibits student loans to young people convicted of any drug offense; all other criminal offenders remain eligible.

This is clearly an overreaction on the part of government. No drug is perfectly safe, and every psychoactive drug can be used in ways that are problematic. The federal government has spent billions of dollars on advertisements and anti-drug programs that preach the dangers of marijuana—that it's a gateway drug, and addictive in its own right, and dramatically more potent than it used to be, and responsible for all sorts of physical and social diseases as well as international terrorism. But the government has yet to repudiate the 1988 finding of the Drug Enforcement Administration's [DEA] own administrative law judge, Francis Young, who concluded after extensive testimony that "marijuana in its natural form is one of the safest therapeutically active substances known to man."

Is marijuana a gateway drug? Yes, insofar as most Americans try marijuana before they try other illicit drugs. But no, insofar as the vast majority of Americans who have tried marijuana have never gone on to try other illegal drugs, much less get in trouble with them, and most have never even gone on to become regular or problem marijuana users. Trying to reduce heroin addiction by preventing marijuana use, it's been said, is like trying to reduce motorcycle fatalities by cracking down on bicycle riding. If marijuana did not exist, there's little reason to believe that there would be less drug abuse in the U.S.; indeed, its role would most likely be filled by a more dangerous substance.

Is marijuana dramatically more potent today? There's certainly a greater variety of high-quality marijuana available today than 30 years ago. But anyone who smoked marijuana in the 1970s and 1980s can recall smoking pot that was just as strong as anything available today. What's more, one needs to take only a few puffs of higher-potency pot to get the desired effect, so there's less wear and tear on the lungs.

Is marijuana addictive? Yes, it can be, in that some people use it to excess, in ways that are problematic for themselves and those around them, and find it hard to stop. But marijuana may well be the least addictive and least damaging of all commonly used psychoactive drugs, including many that are now legal. Most people who smoke marijuana never become dependent. Withdrawal symptoms pale compared with those from other drugs. No one has ever died from a marijuana overdose, which cannot be said of most other drugs. Marijuana is not associated with violent behavior and only minimally with reckless sexual behavior. And even heavy marijuana smokers smoke only a fraction of what cigarette addicts smoke. Lung cancers involving only marijuana are rare.

The government's most recent claim is that marijuana abuse accounts for more people entering treatment than any other illegal drug. That shouldn't be surprising, given that tens of millions of Americans smoke marijuana while only a few million use all other illicit drugs. But the claim is spurious nonetheless. Few Americans who enter "treatment" for marijuana are addicted. Fewer than one in five people entering drug treatment for marijuana do so voluntarily. More than half were referred by the criminal-justice system. They go because they got caught with a joint or failed a drug test at school or work (typically for having smoked marijuana days ago, not for being impaired), or because they were caught by a law-enforcement officer—and attending a marijuana "treatment" program is what's required to avoid expulsion, dismissal, or incarceration. Many traditional drug-treatment programs shamelessly participate in this charade to preserve a profitable and captive client stream.

Even those who recoil at the "nanny state" telling adults what they can or cannot sell to one another often make an exception when it comes to marijuana—to "protect the kids." This is a bad joke, as any teenager will attest. The criminalization of marijuana for adults has not prevented young people from having better access to marijuana than anyone else. Even as marijuana's popularity has waxed and waned since the 1970s, one statistic has remained constant: More than 80 percent of high-school students report it's easy to get. Meanwhile, the government's exaggerations and outright dishonesty easily backfire. For every teen who refrains from trying marijuana because it's illegal (for adults), another is tempted by its status as "forbidden fruit." Many respond to the lies about marijuana by disbelieving warnings about more dangerous drugs. So much for protecting the kids by criminalizing the adults.

The Medical Dimension

The debate over medical marijuana obviously colors the broader debate over marijuana prohibition. Marijuana's medical efficacy is no longer in serious dispute. Its use as a medicine dates back thousands of years. Pharmaceutical products containing marijuana's central ingredient, THC, are legally sold in the U.S., and more are emerging. Some people find the pill form satisfactory, and others consume it in teas or baked products. Most find smoking the easiest and most effective way to consume this unusual medicine, but non-smoking consumption methods, notably vaporizers, are emerging.

Federal law still prohibits medical marijuana. But every state ballot initiative to legalize medical marijuana has been approved, often by wide margins—in California, Washington, Oregon, Alaska, Colorado, Nevada, Maine, and Washington, D.C. State legislatures in Vermont, Hawaii, and Maryland have followed suit, and many others are now considering their own medical-marijuana bills—including New York, Connecticut, Rhode Island, and Illinois. Support is often bipartisan, with Republican governors like Gary Johnson and Maryland's Bob Ehrlich taking the lead. In New York's 2002 gubernatorial campaign, the conservative candidate of the Independence party, Tom Golisano, surprised everyone by campaigning heavily on this issue. The medical-marijuana bill now before the New York legislature is backed not just by leading Republicans but even by some Conservative party leaders.

The political battleground increasingly pits the White House—first under Clinton and now Bush—against everyone else. Majorities in virtually every state in the country would vote, if given the chance, to legalize medical marijuana. Even

Congress is beginning to turn; last summer about two-thirds of House Democrats and a dozen Republicans voted in favor of an amendment co-sponsored by Republican Dana Rohrabacher to prohibit federal funding of any Justice Department crackdowns on medical marijuana in the states that had legalized it. (Many more Republicans privately expressed support, but were directed to vote against.) And federal courts have imposed limits on federal aggression: first in *Conant v. Walters*, which now protects the First Amendment rights of doctors and patients to discuss medical marijuana, and more recently in *Raich v. Ashcroft* and *Santa Cruz v. Ashcroft*, which determined that the federal government's power to regulate interstate commerce does not provide a basis for prohibiting medical-marijuana operations that are entirely local and noncommercial. (The Supreme Court let the *Conant* decision stand, but has yet to consider the others.)

State and local governments are increasingly involved in trying to regulate medical marijuana, notwithstanding the federal prohibition. California, Oregon, Hawaii, Alaska, Colorado, and Nevada have created confidential medical-marijuana patient registries, which protect bona fide patients and caregivers from arrest or prosecution. Some municipal governments are now trying to figure out how to regulate production and distribution. In California, where dozens of medical-marijuana programs now operate openly, with tacit approval by local authorities, some program directors are asking to be licensed and regulated. Many state and local authorities, including law enforcement, favor this but are intimidated by federal threats to arrest and prosecute them for violating federal law.

The drug czar and DEA spokespersons recite the mantra that "there is no such thing as medical marijuana," but the claim is so specious on its face that it clearly undermines federal credibility. The federal government currently provides marijuana—from its own production site in Mississippi—to a few patients who years ago were recognized by the courts as bona fide patients. No one wants to debate those who have used marijuana for medical purposes, be it Santa Cruz medical-marijuana hospice founder Valerie Corral or *National Review*'s Richard Brookhiser. Even many federal officials quietly regret the assault on medical marijuana. When the DEA raided Corral's hospice in September 2002, one agent was heard to say, "Maybe I'm going to think about getting another job sometime soon."

The Broader Movement

The bigger battle, of course, concerns whether marijuana prohibition will ultimately go the way of alcohol Prohibition, replaced by a variety of state and local tax and regulatory policies with modest federal involvement. Dedicated prohibitionists see medical marijuana as the first step down a slippery slope to full legalization. The voters who approved the medical-marijuana ballot initiatives (as well as the wealthy men who helped fund the campaigns) were roughly divided between those who support broader legalization and those who don't, but united in seeing the criminalization and persecution of medical-marijuana patients as the most distasteful aspect of the war on marijuana. (This was a point that Buckley made forcefully in his columns about the plight of Peter McWilliams, who likely died because federal authorities effectively forbade him to use marijuana as medicine.)

The medical-marijuana effort has probably aided the broader anti-prohibitionist campaign in three ways. It helped transform the face of marijuana in the media, from the stereotypical rebel with long hair and tie-dyed shirt to an ordinary middle-aged American struggling with MS or cancer or AIDS. By winning first Proposition 215, the 1996 medical-marijuana ballot initiative in California, and then a string of similar victories in other states, the nascent drug-policy-reform movement demonstrated that it could win in the big leagues of American politics. And the emergence of successful models of medical-marijuana control is likely to boost public confidence in the possibilities and virtue of regulating non-medical use as well.

In this regard, the history of Dutch policy on cannabis (i.e., marijuana and hashish) is instructive. The "coffee shop" model in the Netherlands, where retail (but not wholesale) sale of cannabis is de facto legal, was not legislated into existence. It evolved in fits and starts following the decriminalization of cannabis by Parliament in 1976, as consumers, growers, and entrepreneurs negotiated and collaborated with local police, prosecutors, and other authorities to find an acceptable middle-ground policy. "Coffee shops" now operate throughout the country, subject to local regulations. Troublesome shops are shut down, and most are well integrated into local city cultures. Cannabis is no more popular than in the U.S. and other Western countries, notwithstanding the effective absence of criminal sanctions and controls. Parallel developments are now underway in other countries.

Like the Dutch decriminalization law in 1976, California's Prop 215 in 1996 initiated a dialogue over how best to implement the new law. The variety of outlets that have emerged—ranging from pharmacy-like stores to medical "coffee shops" to hospices, all of which provide marijuana only to people with a patient ID card or doctor's recommendation—play a key role as the most public symbol and manifestation of this dialogue. More such outlets will likely pop up around the country as other states legalize marijuana for medical purposes and then seek ways to regulate distribution and access. And the question will inevitably arise: If the emerging system is successful in controlling production and distribution of marijuana for those with a medical need, can it not also expand to provide for those without medical need?

Millions of Americans use marijuana not just "for fun" but because they find it useful for many of the same reasons that people drink alcohol or take pharmaceutical drugs. It's akin to the beer, glass of wine, or cocktail at the end of the workday, or the prescribed drug to alleviate depression or anxiety, or the sleeping pill, or the aid to sexual function and pleasure. More and more Americans are apt to describe some or all of their marijuana use as "medical" as the definition of that term evolves and broadens. Their anecdotal experiences are increasingly backed by new scientific research into marijuana's essential ingredients, the cannabinoids. Last year, a subsidiary of *The Lancet*, Britain's leading medical journal, speculated whether marijuana might soon emerge as the "aspirin of the 21st century," providing a wide array of medical benefits at low cost to diverse populations.

Perhaps the expansion of the medical-control model provides the best answer—at least in the U.S.—to the question of how best to reduce the substantial costs and harms of marijuana prohibition without inviting significant increases in real drug abuse. It's analogous to the evolution of many pharmaceutical drugs from prescription to over-the-counter, but with stricter controls still in place. It's also an incrementalist approach to reform that can provide both the control and the reassurance that cautious politicians and voters desire.

In 1931, with public support for alcohol Prohibition rapidly waning, President Hoover released the report of the Wickersham Commission. The report included a devastating critique of Prohibition's failures and costly consequences, but the commissioners, apparently fearful of getting out too far ahead of public opinion, opposed repeal. Franklin P. Adams of the *New York World* neatly summed up their findings:

Prohibition is an awful flop.

We like it.

It can't stop what it's meant to stop.

We like it.

It's left a trail of graft and slime

It don't prohibit worth a dime

It's filled our land with vice and crime,

Nevertheless, we're for it.

Two years later, federal alcohol Prohibition was history.

What support there is for marijuana prohibition would likely and quickly absent the billions of dollars spent annually by federal and other governments to prop it up. All those anti-marijuana ads pretend to be about reducing drug abuse, but in fact their basic purpose is sustaining popular support for the war on marijuana. What's needed now are conservative politicians willing to say enough is enough: Tens of billions of taxpayer dollars down the drain each year. People losing their jobs, their property, and their freedom for nothing more than possessing a joint or growing a few marijuana plants. And all for what? To send a message? To keep pretending that we're protecting our children? Alcohol Prohibition made a lot more sense than marijuana prohibition does today—and it, too, was a disaster.

The Positive Economic Impact of Legalization

Quentin Hardy

*Milton Friedman was one of the most influential economic think-
ers of the twentieth century. He won the Nobel Peace Prize for
Economics in 1976 and his theories have had a profound impact
on modern-day economic policy. In the following article published a year before Friedman's death in 2006, Quentin Hardy
reports that the conservative economist endorsed a 2005 Harvard
University report which urges the legalization of marijuana in
the United States for fiscal reasons. Written by economist Jeffrey
A. Miron, the study speculates that federal and state governments could save a combined $7.7 billion by decriminalizing
marijuana; further, they could generate $6.2 billion a year in
new revenue by regulating and taxing the drug. Not only does he
believe that Miron's findings are sound, Hardy writes, but Friedman also states that antidrug laws are too strict and that prohibition enforcement agencies have become corrupt.*

A founding father of the Reagan Revolution has put his
John Hancock on a pro-pot report.

Milton Friedman leads a list of more than 500 economists
from around the U.S. who today [June 2, 2005] will publicly
endorse a Harvard University economist's report on the costs
of marijuana prohibition and the potential revenue gains from
the U.S. government instead legalizing it and taxing its sale.
Ending prohibition enforcement would save $7.7 billion in
combined state and federal spending, the report says, while
taxation would yield up to $6.2 billion a year.

The report, "The Budgetary Implications of Marijuana
Prohibition," (available at: www.prohibitioncosts.org) was

written by Jeffrey A. Miron, a professor at Harvard, and largely paid for by the Marijuana Policy Project (MPP), a Washington, D.C., group advocating the review and liberalization of marijuana laws.

At times the report uses some debatable assumptions: For instance, Miron assumes a single figure for every type of arrest, for example, but the average pot bust is likely cheaper than bringing in a murder or kidnapping suspect. Friedman and other economists, however, say the overall work is some of the best yet done on the costs of the war on marijuana.

At 92, Friedman is revered as one of the great champions of free-market capitalism during the years of U.S. rivalry with Communism. He is also passionate about the need to legalize marijuana, among other drugs, for both financial and moral reasons.

"There is no logical basis for the prohibition of marijuana," the economist says, "$7.7 billion is a lot of money, but that is one of the lesser evils. Our failure to successfully enforce these laws is responsible for the deaths of thousands of people in Colombia. I haven't even included the harm to young people. It's absolutely disgraceful to think of picking up a 22-year-old for smoking pot. More disgraceful is the denial of marijuana for medical purposes."

Securing the signatures of Friedman, along with economists from Cornell, Stanford and Yale universities, among others, is a coup for the MPP, a group largely interested in widening and publicizing debate over the usefulness of laws against pot.

If the laws change, large beneficiaries might include large agricultural groups like Archer Daniels Midland and ConAgra Foods as potential growers or distributors and liquor businesses like Constellation Brands and Allied Domecq, which understand the distribution of intoxicants. Surprisingly, Home Depot and other home gardening centers would not particularly benefit, according to the report, which projects that few people would grow their own marijuana, the same way few people distill whiskey at home. Canada's large-scale domestic marijuana growing industry suggests otherwise, however.

The report will likely not sway all minds. The White House Office of Drug Control Policy recently published an analysis of marijuana incarceration that states that "most people in prison for marijuana are violent criminals, repeat offenders, traffickers or all of the above." The office declined to comment on the marijuana economics study, however, without first analyzing the study's methodology.

Friedman's advocacy on the issue is limited—the nonagenarian prefers to write these days on the need for school choice, calling U.S. literacy levels "absolutely criminal . . . only sustained because of the power of the teachers' unions." Yet his thinking on legalizing drugs extends well past any MPP debate or the kind of liberalization favored by most advocates.

"I've long been in favor of legalizing all drugs," he says, but not because of the standard libertarian arguments for unrestricted personal freedom. "Look at the factual consequences: The harm done and the corruption created by these laws . . . the costs are one of the lesser evils."

Not that a man of his years expects reason to triumph. Any added revenues from taxing legal marijuana would almost certainly be more than spent, by this or any other Congress.

"Deficits are the only thing that keeps this Congress from spending more" says Friedman. "Republicans are no different from Democrats. Spending is the easiest way to buy votes." A sober assessment indeed.

Legalized Marijuana Will Make Lazy Kids Even Lazier

Steve Sailer

In the following article Steve Sailer considers the social ramifications of legalizing marijuana in the United States. He points out that kids are too passive today because they watch too much TV, play too many video games, and eat too much food. Sailer also criticizes parents who carefully schedule their kids' activities and who do not send them outside to find creative things to do on their own. He concludes that legalizing marijuana will make already-lazy kids even lazier.

In Quentin Tarantino's *Jackie Brown*, Samuel L. Jackson comes home to find Bridget Fonda lying on the couch, smoking dope, and giggling at the TV. Disgusted, he tells her that marijuana will rob her of her ambitions.

"Not if your ambition is to get high and watch TV," she replies.

Smoking Pot Saps Kids' Energy

It's fashionable among conservative and libertarian journalists, such as the editors of *National Review* and *Reason* magazines, to demand the decriminalization or legalization of drugs, especially of marijuana.

Many weighty arguments have been mobilized in support of this cause. Yet this movement has only made fitful progress in the quarter of a century since the first generation of American voters to have much first-hand experience with marijuana began to have children themselves. Parents now understand that additional marijuana use would exacerbate many of the unhealthy and unfulfilling trends already at work in our society.

Steve Sailer, "The Kids Are Alwrong," *The American Spectator*, September 7, 2004. Copyright © *The American Spectator* 2004. Reproduced by permission.

The problem with marijuana is not that it's some wild and crazy thing, but that it's middle-age-in-a-bong. Smoking dope saps the energy from youth, turning them into sedentary couch potatoes.

The parents of America already have a hard enough time getting their teenagers—and, increasingly, their adult children who have come back home to live—off the TV room floor when they are perfectly straight. Parents understand that changing laws to make marijuana more readily available—and, let's not kid ourselves, that's what these "reforms" would do—would create an even more inert and obese generation of young people.

Smoking dope may not do all that many of the horrible things often attributed to it, but it definitely makes people want to sit down. And that's something even the most clean and sober young people of the 21st Century do way too much of already.

Whenever parents get together, the talk eventually turns to how Kids These Days—including perfectly adjusted ones—never want to go outside. Sunshine is their enemy. Everything they desire most in life—100 channels, video games, instant messaging—comes to them on a screen, best viewed in a darkened room.

Kids Are Already Too Distracted by Technology

Marijuana also makes people easily amused. In an electronic age, where an unlimited supply of entertainment is instantly available around the clock, that's not a good thing. It's hard enough to for young people to decide that they shouldn't spend another twenty minutes flipping through the cable TV dial once again on the assumption that—while all the programs the last six times around were lame—something cool has got to have come on in the meantime. Add THC to their brain chemistry and they're headed for an infinite loop.

Eventually, marijuana-augmented TV addiction becomes a very real threat to getting anything done in life. The last thing parents want is for their children is for them to wind up like that perpetually baked stoner The Dude ("or El Duderino if you're not into the whole brevity thing") played by Jeff Bridges in *The Big Lebowski*.

Parents Today Are Raising More Passive Kids

It's not just technology's fault. The way middle class parents now raise their kids can incline them toward passivity, which the availability of marijuana can horribly aggravate.

Another reason kids don't go outside anymore is because leaving the house has become an enormous production number. When I had a baseball game as a kid, I merely grabbed my glove and walked or biked to the park. No trouble.

My son's adolescent teammates, in contrast, never arrive for their league games in anything less massive than a Ford Explorer, because the crime rate is too scary for their parents to let them walk and the traffic too dense for them to pedal. Further, they have to lug not only a duffel bag full of baseball impedimenta, but at least one, and preferably, both parents, lest they grow up to write self-pitying screenplays about how nobody ever came to watch them play.

Not surprisingly, the concept of spontaneously heading over to the park between scheduled games to see who wants to play some ball seems to modern suburban boys to be as outdated and unfeasible an idea for having fun as tipping cows.

Growing up in a world where every activity is carefully scheduled by parents means fewer youths are self-starters. They don't expect to initiate activity. They take the same attitude toward free time as do soldiers in a hurry-up-and-wait Army: unless somebody in command is yelling at them to do something, they don't do anything. They just flop down and try to amuse themselves in the meantime. More marijuana would only make this already inactive lifestyle worse.

Not surprisingly, young Americans have gotten fatter and fatter as the proliferation of remote controls means they don't even have to walk across the room anymore to turn up the stereo. Believe me: the munchies aren't going to make *that* problem any better.

Marijuana Could Provide a New Revenue Source for States

David Lazarus

Observing that California had a budget deficit of $17.5 billion in 2002, David Lazarus argues that legalizing and taxing marijuana could create a lucrative new source of revenue for the economically ailing state. Based on projections indicating that California's annual marijuana crop is worth about $4 billion, Lazarus proposes that taxing the crop could generate revenue of anywhere from $317 million to $2.1 billion, depending on the aggressiveness of the regulation. While Lazarus acknowledges prohibitionists' concerns about the potential proliferation of marijuana if it were legalized, he cites the opinions of a number of authorities who contend that decriminalizing the drug will not necessarily lead to increased use, particularly among minors.

With the state Legislature's chief budget analyst saying that California is now [March 2002] $17.5 billion in the red, only two choices exist to get us out of this fix: deep cuts in spending or finding new revenue sources.

Perhaps it's time for serious consideration to be given to legalizing California's biggest cash crop—marijuana.

I know, I know. Just bringing up the topic is going to set alarm bells ringing in some quarters. Let's try to contain our emotions for just a minute and look at this issue from a purely public-policy and economic perspective.

Pot advocates say it has already been found to have medical benefits. In 1996, voters statewide approved Proposition 215, the Compassionate Use Act, legalizing marijuana for medicinal purposes.

David Lazarus, "State's Untapped Pot of Gold," *San Francisco Chronicle*, March 1, 2002. © 2002 San Francisco Chronicle. Republished with permission of *San Francisco Chronicle*, conveyed through Copyright Clearance Center, Inc.

But higher-ups in Washington have since decided that federal anti-drug laws take precedence over state measures and are thus cracking down on organizations that seek to make life easier for people with AIDS cancer or other ailments.

Beyond the clear medical advantages, though, pot could have an enormous impact on the struggling California economy, provided the feds allowed the state to go down that road.

A 1998 report by the National Organization for the Reform of Marijuana Laws determined that American dope growers earn more than $15 billion annually on the wholesale market. Only corn, soybeans and hay are more profitable cash crops.

The annual marijuana crop in California is worth about $4 billion, the organization found, making it the state's single-most-lucrative agricultural resource—more than the production value of grapes and almonds combined.

Daniel Sumner, an agricultural economist at the University of California at Davis, noted that a considerable portion of pot's current cash value lies in its illegal status. Buyers are forced to subsidize growers' security measures.

Sumner said marijuana's status as the state's largest cash crop would almost certainly come to an end under legalization as growing costs fall in line with similar crops, such as tobacco.

As a revenue source, however, he said dope could have a profound impact on state coffers. Like tobacco, legalized marijuana could be expected to be sold retail with hefty taxes attached.

Sumner speculated that as much as a 1,000 percent tax on marijuana might be levied to keep retail costs sufficiently high and thus deter use by minors.

"It makes more sense to tax things than to ban them," he said. "You generate revenue and you give people an incentive to behave the way we want."

Sheri Larsen, a spokeswoman for the California Board of Equalization, said that if an 8 percent sales tax were levied on a $4 billion marijuana crop, the state would take in an extra $317 million a year.

But that number is only a fraction of the revenue that would be expected if Sumner is correct about a whopping dope tax. The 87-cents-per-pack tax on cigarettes, for example, produced $1.1 billion in revenue for California last year [2001].

If the almost 53 percent tax now levied on cigars and other tobacco products were applied to a $4 billion marijuana crop, this would result in $2.1 billion in revenue.

Of course, no law or tax by itself is going to keep kids from experimenting with forbidden fruit. Researchers at Columbia University reported last week that teenagers now account for about a quarter of all alcohol consumed in the United States.

Meanwhile, the U.S. Department of Health and Human Services says marijuana use by teens has leveled off. About 15 percent of eighth-graders, 33 percent of 10th-graders and 37 percent of 12th-graders tried pot last year [2001], the department found.

Yet those who argue that keeping marijuana illegal keeps it out of the hands of youngsters should look at the health department's statistics for cigarette use.

About 12 percent of eighth-graders, 21 percent of 10th-graders and nearly 30 percent of 12th-graders smoked cigarettes last year—almost identical levels as marijuana use.

Kind of makes you wonder if teens would smoke even less dope if some of the mystique of the drug were stripped away by decriminalization.

As for adults, a nationwide poll in December [2001] by Zogby International found that in light of post-Sept. 11 security concerns, 61 percent oppose arresting and jailing nonviolent marijuana smokers.

It is, of course, a stretch to think that lawmakers, either at the state or federal level, would risk their political necks on an issue like this. You can just imagine how they'd get pounded by conservatives.

Robert MacCoun, a professor of public policy and law at the University of California at Berkeley, spent 10 years studying worldwide drug policies. He concluded in the book *Drug War Heresies* (co-authored with economist Peter Reuter) that removing penalties for marijuana does not lead to increased use.

The only way use of legalized pot would significantly increase, MacCoun told me, would be if dope smoking was aggressively promoted by profit-hungry corporations, a la the tobacco industry.

If advertising could be restricted, he said, "it's hard to show social harm from widespread marijuana use."

Me, I'm kind of conflicted. I don't do drugs anymore—haven't for many years—but I did smoke pot back in college, and must say I enjoyed it quite a bit.

I never regarded dope as anywhere near as harmful or dangerous as alcohol or cigarettes, and certainly nowhere in the same league as harder drugs.

It's only a matter of time, though, before my young son confronts the temptations of the world, and I have to be honest when I say I'd prefer he didn't mess with any mood-altering substances. I'm not yet sure what I'm going to tell him.

But I do agree with UC Davis' Sumner that taxation and regulation are far more effective tools than prohibition in keeping people from indulging in vices.

Keeping marijuana illegal just doesn't make sense. And for a state that grows tons of it, and which can't pay its bills, legalization might at last be a very smart move indeed.

Marijuana Legalization Needs Honest Debate

Jon Gettman

Jon Gettman is a regular contributor to High Times *and a former national director of the National Organization for the Reform of Marijuana Laws (NORML). Here, he argues that marijuana legalization advocates should have an open, honest dialogue with the public about their motives for wanting to decriminalize the drug. According to Gettman, it is okay for pro-marijuana activists to admit that they like to smoke pot, but they must then reassure the public that they will engage in responsible use and conduct if marijuana is legalized.*

Ask advocates why they want marijuana legalized and they will provide a variety of answers but rarely will they admit the obvious: they like marijuana.

It's not that marijuana legalization advocates are ashamed of cannabis but that they've been trained to discuss the issue in the abstract by public interest groups who operate in constant fear of being labeled "pro-marijuana" or otherwise being tagged as promoting marijuana use instead of political reform.

Most of the public understand that many people use or have used marijuana without serious consequences for personal or public health. The public also understands that many marijuana users favor legalization because they like pot and don't want to be arrested for it. It's pretty obvious, and the public is skeptical of advocates who try to pretend otherwise.

When asked the question most advocates attempt to address the issue in terms of the public interest. The usual answers to the legalization question are in the 2nd person or 3rd person, as in here's why you should want it legalized (2nd person) and here's why society should want it legalized (3rd person). These answers, reasonable as they are avoid the question. They are evasive, they avoid the 1st person response, as in why do I want marijuana legalized.

Here is an example of a direct, first person, answer: I want to be able to grow and use marijuana legally as an alternative to alcohol, and to do so I am willing to pay taxes, cooperate with a regulated market, support other drug control efforts, and promote socially responsible conduct.

Debate the Issue Honestly

People use marijuana for different reasons, and answers to the question will vary considerably. What's important, though, is not so much the reason for wanting legalization but instead what one is willing to offer society in order to get it.

The legalization of marijuana will not be achieved through cleverness; it is not a matter of refining an argument or implementing a shrewd public relations campaign. Legalization is a political objective, and political objectives are accomplished through making deals, through an agreed upon exchange of actions. Deals, though, ultimately require trust, something marijuana users are quite familiar with. Honesty builds trust, and more honesty about marijuana use in the United States can only advance the cause of legalization.

Honesty about marijuana use reassures the public that marijuana does not have a high potential for abuse, indeed one of the symptoms of long-term use of a drug with a high potential for abuse is to avoid honest discussion about it. Honesty about the personal interest of advocates in legalization also builds credibility when it comes to the more important issue of socially responsible conduct. Politics is not only primarily a local phenomenon; it's a personal one as well. This is as much a matter between "we the people" as it is a matter between the people and their government. The latter struggle is often a matter of rights, but when it comes to deriving a social compact that provides the basis for a political consensus producing the legalization of marijuana it is a matter of discussing responsibilities and obligations rather than rights and entitlements.

Engaging in Responsible Conduct

Marijuana users are responsible individuals, and avoiding discussion of their interest in using marijuana also avoids opportunities to discuss their interest in being responsible citizens. The public is a lot more interested in responsible conduct than they are responsible use. Using drugs responsibly is a matter of self-interest for most of the public, they believe that if someone is careless enough to use drugs irresponsibly they deserve whatever trouble it causes.

Responsible conduct, though, is a different matter than responsible use. Certainly the public is interested in hearing about the impact of legalization on personal conduct involving such matters as safety (driving under the influence) and restricted availability (not providing marijuana to teenagers and children). Many parents are just as concerned, though, about marijuana use in public, whether it is otherwise responsible use or not. The attitude of many parents can be generally summarized as "please, not in front of the kids", underscoring their concern over the conduct of marijuana users over any concern for the effects on the users themselves. Most marijuana users view it as a private matter anyway, just as most marijuana users engage in responsible conduct whether they are stoned or not.

So, it's okay to like pot, and if you want to argue in favor of marijuana's legalization it's okay to talk about your personal interest in this issue. Just remember there is a difference between one's personal interest, the personal interest of others, and the overall public interest. Sounds complicated, but it's not. It's just a matter of offering the same respect for others that marijuana users should demand for themselves.

Considering the Public Interest

Arguments for legalizing marijuana should consist of two parts, why the advocate is in favor of it and why the audience should be. Advocates of marijuana legalization need to state both their personal interest in the issue and what actions they will take, personally, to address the audience's interests. This serves the public interest because consensus is one of the results of this sort of compact-building approach.

You can't begin work on a social compact, though, without first making it an issue for discussion. The best way to begin that process is for marijuana users to begin to address the issue in the first person, to claim a personal stake in the outcome of public debate over the marijuana laws, and to directly contradict the widespread misimpression that marijuana users are not socially responsible citizens.

Being direct about a personal interest in marijuana's legalization, though, does not require an admission of past or present violations of the law. Note that the example above does not state "I use marijuana" or that "I have used marijuana illegally" but, rather, asserts that "I want to use marijuana legally." Again, one has to look at it as a proposal, as a prospective deal, in the future I want to do this and I am willing to do this in return.

Adopting a Better Policy

Everyone understands that many people now use marijuana illegally. That's the point. Legalizing marijuana is not about validating that use; it's not about saying it was okay for people to break the marijuana laws because it turns out there's a better way to regulate it. Legalizing marijuana is simply about society adopting the better way, and what makes it a better way of regulation is the one thing that marijuana users have to offer in exchange for it, their cooperation in making regulation a more successful policy than the current prohibition.

The public is a lot more receptive to legalizing marijuana than ever before. It's time for marijuana users to address the issue in the first person, it's time for advocates of legalization to explain their personal stake in the issue, and it's time to use honesty about marijuana use and social responsibility as a way to achieve legalization through building consensus rather than through inciting confrontation and divisiveness. It's okay to like pot, but ultimately marijuana use is about consciousness, consciousness is about responsibility, and responsibility requires an honest compact between marijuana users and the rest of society.

CHAPTER 4

Marijuana and
the War on Drugs

Marijuana Becomes the Primary Target of Drug War in the 1990s

Dan Eggen

The Sentencing Project, a Washington DC–based think tank that advocates reassessing traditional approaches to incarceration, released a study in 2005 that documents a precipitous increase in marijuana arrests in the 1990s, while arrests for hard drugs like heroin and cocaine decreased during the same time frame. According to Dan Eggen, the study found that marijuana arrests— mostly for possession as opposed to distribution—rose from 28 percent to 45 percent of all drug arrests from 1992 to 2002; by contrast, arrests for hard drugs fell from a high of 55 percent to less than 30 percent over the same period. Government officials maintain that the drug war's focus on marijuana is not the result of any concerted enforcement effort, Eggen writes; rather, it reflects a natural response to rising trends in marijuana production and use in the late twentieth century.

The focus of the drug war in the United States has shifted significantly over the past decade from hard drugs to marijuana, which now accounts for nearly half of all drug arrests nationwide, according to an analysis of federal crime statistics released yesterday [May 3, 2005].

The study of FBI data by a Washington-based think tank, the Sentencing Project, found that the proportion of heroin and cocaine cases plummeted from 55 percent of all drug arrests in 1992 to less than 30 percent 10 years later. During the same period, marijuana arrests rose from 28 percent of the total to 45 percent.

Coming in the wake of the focus on crack cocaine in the late 1980s, the increasing emphasis on marijuana enforcement was accompanied by a dramatic rise in overall drug arrests, from fewer than 1.1 million in 1990 to more than 1.5 million a decade later. Eighty percent of that increase came from marijuana arrests, the study found.

The rapid increase has not had a significant impact on prisons, however, because just 6 percent of the arrests resulted in felony convictions, the study found. The most widely quoted household survey on the topic has shown relatively little change in the overall rate of marijuana use over the same time period, experts said.

"In reality, the war on drugs as pursued in the 1990s was to a large degree a war on marijuana," said Ryan S. King, the study's co-author and a research associate at the Sentencing Project. "Marijuana is the most widely used illegal substance, but that doesn't explain this level of growth over time. . . . The question is, is this really where we want to be spending all our money?"

The think tank is a left-leaning group that advocates alternatives to traditional imprisonment. Criminologists and government officials confirmed the trend, which in some ways marks a return to a previous era. In 1982, marijuana arrests accounted for 72 percent of all drug arrests, according to the study.

Government Justifies Emphasis on Marijuana

Bush administration officials attribute the rise in marijuana arrests to a variety of factors: increased use among teenagers during parts of the 1990s; efforts by local police departments to focus more on street-level offenses; and growing concerns over the danger posed by modern, more potent versions of marijuana. The White House Office of National Drug Control Policy released a study yesterday [May 3, 2005] showing that youth who use marijuana are more likely to develop serious mental health problems, including depression and schizophrenia.

"This is not Cheech and Chong marijuana," said David Murray, a policy analyst for the anti-drug office. "It's a qualitatively different drug, and that's reflected in the numbers."

The new statistics come amid signs of a renewed debate in political circles over the efficacy of U.S. drug policies, which have received less attention recently amid historically low crime rates and a focus on terrorism since the Sept. 11, 2001, attacks. Attorney General Alberto R. Gonzales, for example, has formed a national committee to oversee prosecution of violent drug gangs and has vowed to focus more resources on the fight against methamphetamine manufacturers and other drug traffickers.

Critics Find Marijuana Emphasis Unfair

But increasingly, some experts have begun to argue that the U.S. drug war, which costs an estimated $35 billion a year, has had a minimal impact on consumption of illicit substances. The conservative American Enterprise Institute published a report in March [2005] titled "Are We Losing the War on Drugs?" Its authors argue that, among other things, "criminal punishment of marijuana use does not appear to be justified."

The study released yesterday by the Sentencing Project found that arrests for marijuana account for nearly all of the increase in drug arrests seen during the 1990s. The report also found that one in four people in state prisons for marijuana offenses can be classified as a "low-level offender," and it estimated that $4 billion a year is spent on arresting and prosecuting marijuana crimes.

In addition, the study showed that although African Americans make up 14 percent of marijuana users generally, they account for nearly a third of all marijuana arrests.

Among the most striking findings was the researchers' examination of arrest trends in New York City, which focused intently on "zero tolerance" policies during Rudolph W. Giuliani's mayoral administration [from 1994 to 2002]. Marijuana arrests in the city increased tenfold from 1990 to 2002, from 5,100 to more than 50,000, the report said. Nine of 10 of arrests in 2002 were for possession rather than dealing.

The study also found a wide disparity in the growth of marijuana arrests in some of the United States' largest counties, from a 20 percent increase in San Diego to a 418 percent spike in King County, Wash. (The only decrease in the sample came in Northern Virginia's Fairfax County, where marijuana arrests declined by 37 percent.)

"There's been a major change in what's going on in drug enforcement, but it clearly isn't something that someone set out to do," said Jonathan Caulkins, a criminology professor at Carnegie Mellon University in Pittsburgh. "It's not like anyone said, 'We don't care about cocaine and heroin anymore'.... The simple answer may be that police are now taking opportunities to make more marijuana arrests than they were when they were focused on crack cocaine in the 1980s."

Logic Must Frame
the Marijuana Debate

Mitch Earleywine

Mitch Earleywine is a leading authority on the scientific study of marijuana use and abuse. In the following article, he states that implementing a viable marijuana policy depends on establishing a logical and rational debate between prohibitionists and reformers. Earleywine identifies a number of erroneous or poorly conceived arguments that prohibitionists and reformers have made to emphasize their positions on marijuana use, including overgeneralization, jumping to conclusions, and emotional reasoning. He advocates the implementation of twelve questions that one should ask before debating marijuana policy in an effort to frame the discussion impartially and logically.

Few people realize that they have been misled about marijuana, marijuana policy, and the effects of both on their lives. Hundreds of millions of people have never even seen marijuana and believe they don't know anyone who has used it, but marijuana policy still affects them. Supporters and detractors of marijuana prohibition agree that the plant and the policies designed to control it generate costs. Both sides of the prohibition argument would like to see the plant remain out of the hands of children. Both sides want to ensure that no one drives while impaired. Both sides want problem users of any drug to receive help. Both want to see anyone with a medical condition receive appropriate, inexpensive treatment. Both sides want to end these troubles without sacrificing civil rights, respect for the law, or quality of life. The question is:

How? Resources are limited. The medical, ethical, religious, legal, and economic issues surrounding marijuana policy are remarkably complex.

Even those who have never given marijuana policy much thought would agree that the only way to think about it is to think clearly. Most of us lean a bit toward change or a bit toward the status quo. Many others have strong feelings about tightening enforcement and increasing penalties or dropping prohibition completely. All tend to agree, though, that logical arguments are the best. Those who've seen the discourse on this topic also agree that it's riddled with illogical arguments. Although rationality may not be the answer to every human problem, troubles related to marijuana policy would surely benefit from the judicious use of reason.

A huge volume of research supports the idea that certain critical errors in thinking lead to depression, as we have suspected for more than 40 years. Unfortunately, some of these errors have crept into the debate on marijuana laws, leaving proponents of new laws as well as fans of the status quo feeling less vital and energetic than they might. The first step to improving arguments (and moods) requires identifying these errors with genuine vigilance. No one is immune to these. Many of the errors here come directly from the work of depression researchers, but their application to policy arguments is striking. This list is hardly exhaustive, but the few mistakes detailed here are certainly rampant. Eliminating these glitches in logic will improve the debate on marijuana policy and restore the verve of many people who care so much about this important topic.

Overgeneralizing from Individual Cases

The first error concerns taking a single example as if it were proof of a worldwide trend.

"I know a man who smoked pot once and died of a heart attack!"

"I know a man who smokes pot every day, and he's a millionaire!"

Both prohibitionists and reformers have learned that the public responds to memorable stories of individuals. A graphic tale about one real person grips audiences more than a superb longitudinal study of hundreds. Nevertheless, a single case is a poor argument that marijuana serves as a cause. To prove that marijuana causes any result, we need association, temporal antecedence, and isolation. We have to show an association between marijuana and the result, show that marijuana use preceded the result, and rule out all other potential causes by isolating marijuana as the lone source of the result. Only a large experiment with randomly assigned participants can support a causal argument. Huge samples of people chosen at random to either use the plant regularly or abstain completely might answer some of the central questions that appear and reappear in the policy debate.

Individual cases cannot prove that marijuana creates any result. A single marijuana user is not proof that marijuana either impairs or enhances accomplishments. Thus, any references to individual users, no matter how famous or notorious, can only serve as examples. Since at least a third of Americans have tried the drug at least once, it should be no surprise that many well-known folks, from philanthropists to criminals, have used the plant. The best way to avoid this error may be to emphasize that no single case can generalize to all cases. If every salient example contained this caveat, we'd make some progress. If we reasoned from large experiments instead of individual cases, we could start an intelligent, rational conversation about policy.

Biased Sampling

An error related to overgeneralizing concerns biased sampling. It's easy to assume that information about a select group of accomplished recreational users or troubled addicts applies to the whole world. People for and against new policy have fallen into this trap. I recently spoke at an anti-prohibition gathering with a very brave physician who emphasized that adolescents can run into problems with the plant. One member of the audience turned to the others and said, "How many of you successful people started smoking in your teens?" Of course, the question led to wild applause, but this dramatic demonstration is no proof of marijuana's harmlessness. The users who have troubles with the plant simply weren't in the audience.

Prohibitionists make the same error. Many point to large groups of recovering addicts and say, "How many of you started with marijuana?" But again, this biased sample neglects the millions of people who have used the plant without negative consequence. The only way to establish rates of harm or benefit from the plant requires large samples that include a whole range of folks from all walks of life. Such studies show that 9 out of 10 users do not have problems in their use of marijuana. The same steps for avoiding problems with individual cases apply here as well: Acknowledge the limitations of our samples, and we can have a rational discussion.

Arguing That "It's Natural" Won't Advance Your Argument

The occasional argument for marijuana's harmlessness rests on the idea that the plant is a simple part of nature that requires no processing or alteration for its use. Therefore, it must be innocuous. This approach shows poor reasoning, and anti-prohibitionists should turn to data documenting marijuana's safety rather than resort to such an argument. Poisonous plants are numerous and deadly despite their natural, unadulterated, unprocessed state. The Death Cap mushroom (*Amanita palloides*), hemlock, and mistletoe all serve as examples of toxic plants that should put this argument to rest. In addition, many synthesized medicines have few negative effects despite being unavailable in anyone's backyard.

All-or-Nothing Thinking

As I've mentioned elsewhere, decisions are easier when everything is black and white. Some things really are horrible, and others really are splendid, but most fall in-between. Fire warms some and burns others. Aspirin heals pain or damages livers. Marijuana really is a source of joy for some and trouble for others. Almost every potential marijuana policy has advantages and disadvantages. Where the debate runs into trouble is when a single pro or con is considered reason to dismiss an entire proposal. Few laws are perfect. That's why we can change them. The tacit assumption that any policy must bring us divine perfection or else it is an egregious mistake will drive us all crazy. The best way to dispute this error may require consistent emphasis that some areas are gray rather than all black or all white. We all must be particularly vigilant to catch this type of reasoning in our own arguments.

Jumping to Conclusions

A small but extremely vocal set of debaters often leaps from one simple idea to extreme assertions without any genuine support for their arguments. Both sides fall for this error. Prohibitionists often claim that after decriminalization, marijuana will be sold next to the candy bars at the corner store. Reformers sometimes claim that current laws will soon force a third of Americans into jail. Assertions like these make great sound bites for brief media reports, but these leaps are no way to decide the fate of a nation. Disputing this error requires asking simple questions about how one step leads to the next. How would decriminalization lead to marijuana in a candy store? How would prohibition imprison a third of America? Walking through these steps will reveal the absurdity of these assertions, and help avoid these jumps to conclusions.

Several notorious "slippery slope" arguments fall into this category of jumping to conclusions. I once heard a former Drug Enforcement Administration agent assert that if cannabis becomes legal, the next generation will want Ecstasy to be legal, and soon we'll have a generation that wants heroin legal. He implied that all Americans would soon be opiate addicts. Note how this argument leaps from one topic to the next as if the jumps are simple, logical progressions, when in fact they aren't simple at all. Altering cannabis laws may make voters question policies about other drugs, and I'm happy to list this outcome among the pros and cons of the policy. Nevertheless, assuming that changing cannabis laws will lead to a nation of opiate addicts is simply too far a jump.

Confusing Correlates with Causes

A great many conclusions about drugs are actually erroneous misunderstandings based on simple correlations. It's perfectly human to think that if two things go together, one must have caused the other, but proof of causality requires more than that. One of my favorite examples concerns the correlation between the number of churches in a city and the city's crime rate. Churches and crime correlate highly across U.S. cities. The more churches, the more crime. But churches don't cause crime. Being a victim of a crime doesn't even inspire a lot of folks to open a church. In fact, a third variable accounts for this association: the size of the city. As cities get bigger, they have more crime and more churches. Neither causes the other.

Note how this ridiculous example of confusing correlation for cause seems obvious, but when the same correlation fits our stereotypes, it's harder to recognize the error. People who drink more alcohol also have more unsafe sex. Here's a correlation that seems to cry out for a causal explanation. Yes, it must be that these people get drunk and forget to use a condom. We all can conceive how alcohol can do that. Nevertheless, a close look at individual sexual events reveals that this intuitively appealing causal explanation isn't true. People who like to drink a lot happen to have unsafe sex, but they don't seem to get drunk and then do it. The unsafe sex doesn't seem to occur any more often after drinking than not after drinking. Clearly, some sort of personal preference for taking risks must account for the two behaviors, just as the size of the city accounts for the link between crime and churches.

The confusion of correlation and cause gets particularly insidious with arguments for the so-called "gateway theory." The mistaken notion that marijuana creates an urge for hard drugs the way eating salt makes people thirsty has no support from research. Unfortunately, a study in the *Journal of the American Medical Association* has been misinterpreted to suggest that marijuana causes hard drug use. A close look at the study tells a very different story.

Australian researchers found 311 pairs of same-sex twins in which one had tried marijuana before age 17 but the other had not. The fact that the researchers studied twins is a bit of a red herring. Whether the twins were identical or fraternal, the ones who tried marijuana early were more likely to try other drugs and develop drug problems later in life. If we believe that these data mean that marijuana causes hard drug use, we're sadly mistaken. (The authors of the research even say so, with considerable emphasis.) The analyses actually reveal that early tobacco and alcohol use were also significant predictors of drug problems. Undoubtedly, most people use these legal substances before marijuana. They're simply more available. But the idea that these legal drugs are the gateway never appears in the study or in the subsequent hullabaloo in the media.

In addition, anyone who used a hard drug before using marijuana was dropped from the analyses. That's right. People who took downers or snorted cocaine before they tried marijuana, or did anything else counter to the gateway theory, were omitted from the study. Other research shows that as many as a third of people in treatment for drug problems used hard drugs before they used marijuana. But in short, the deck was stacked so that the gateway theory couldn't be disproved.

Whatever led one twin to try marijuana early also contributed to the other results. The study does not reveal what would make teens try marijuana when their identical twins would not. Obviously, it's not genetics, given that they have the same genes. Nevertheless, anyone who knows identical twins will attest that they are not two copies of the same person. One source of the difference might be the same risk-taking personality discussed with alcohol and unsafe sex. Risk takers like to ride in the front of the roller-coaster, parachute from airplanes, and experiment with drugs. The trait is not completely heritable, and it may account for why one person might smoke marijuana before his or her identical twin. The fact that some people use marijuana early in life and later develop drug problems probably says more about people than it says about marijuana. We all know troubled souls who use a lot of different drugs, drive without seatbelts, have unsafe sex, and engage in a lot of other deviant behaviors. The marijuana does not cause their use of other drugs. They simply use marijuana first because it's the most available substance. In fact, in neighborhoods where crack is more available than marijuana, they use crack first. Surely no one thinks that crack is a gateway drug to marijuana.

The only way to combat this confusion is to require that any purported cause not only correlate with a purported outcome, but also precede it and separate completely from all other potential causes. A step in the right direction would include reanalyzing the Lynskey data while including the participants who used a hard drug before they used marijuana. I'm not going to hold my breath waiting for that to happen.

Unprovable Arguments

A great many assertions in drug policy debates can neither be proved nor disproved. "Legalization sends the wrong message to our youth" and "marijuana liberates the spirit" serve as prime examples. Both of these statements would require some extensive definitions before evidence could offer any support.

What makes a message wrong? (And as I age, I can't help but wonder, who are "our youth"?) What does it mean to liberate the spirit? These assertions can't be disputed or verified because they rely on vague ideas. The only way to proceed with any clarity is to define terms precisely. The only defense against assertions like these may be a simple question: "What does that mean?"

Unfortunately, asking folks to define their terms has become some kind of symbol of ignorance. In a recent debate I heard a prohibitionist assert that marijuana "corrupts the moral fiber of youth." When I asked what that meant, the speaker rolled his eyes in disdain, as if my question were proof that I had no moral fiber. I have seen anti-prohibitionists make comparable gaffs, particularly when they assert that they can't explain marijuana's benefits to anyone who hasn't tried it. The solution to this problem is also quite simple: Define terms. We can't understand each other's arguments unless we define our terms.

Emotional Reasoning

The prime example of emotional reasoning is "I feel it, so it must be so." Marijuana policy stirs a lot of strong feelings, but the feelings are no indicator of right or wrong. Our feelings about this very fact can tell a great deal. Just the idea that our emotions aren't accurate indicators of the truth can make some people angry as hell. The feelings can serve as superb motivators to take action; the anger, frustration, sadness, or disgust anyone experiences in response to any situation can be a great indicator that changes are necessary. But the feelings alone are not a sufficient ground for national policy.

This error gets particularly troublesome in arguments that purport to be moral. Former drug czar William Bennett uses moral expirations in his work. "The simple fact is that drug use is wrong. And the moral argument, in the end, is the most compelling argument." The ironies of Mr. Bennett's own life aside [Bennett reportedly lost millions in high-stakes gambling], I assume he means that the use of intoxicating drugs is wrong. (I doubt he's upset about the morality of aspirin or coffee.) The reasons marijuana consumption is wrong often rely on incontestable ethical insight. When asked what, exactly, is wrong with drug use, prohibitionists frequently fall into circular arguments that cannot be disproved. Drug use is wrong because it is immoral; it is immoral because it is wrong. They sometimes turn to other unfalsifiable ideas as evidence. "Drug use is wrong because it drains the human spirit," or some such thing. These arguments often allude to the negative consequences of drugs, leading one to wonder if drug use would still be immoral if it did not lead to problems. When pressed, many state flatly that drug use feels wrong, so it must be wrong. This argument is emotional reasoning incarnate.

Reformers make comparable errors. I've said myself: "It is wrong for anyone to go to jail for owning a plant." But what, exactly, is wrong? I can spin an argument about how punishments should be proportional to the severity of the crime. But the point is that I can't simply argue that something is wrong because I feel it is wrong, or even because many people feel it is. And though it certainly feels wrong to me, the feeling is not enough. There must be a genuine argument, not just a feeling.

Confusing the Effects of Prohibition with the Effects of Marijuana

Many arguments about marijuana policy confuse the effects of marijuana with the effects of laws. Legal policies cause outcomes that are not the effect of any drug. For example, in a legislative hearing in a state that was considering altering its policies, a law enforcement officer mentioned the shooting deaths of four members of the Royal Canadian Mounted Police as they raided a marijuana field. The tacit assumption behind mention of these deaths was that marijuana caused this violence. Marijuana intoxication does not increase aggression, and it's unclear if those who shot these officers had used the plant. In fact, prohibition created illegal marijuana fields. Just as alcohol prohibition created enormous jumps in murder rates in the United States in the 1920s and early 1930s, prohibition of other drugs has led to tremendous potential for profits and accompanying competition for market share that includes violence. A licit market, taxed and regulated, has the potential to minimize confrontations between police and criminals, as well as hostile turf wars between underground dealers.

The solution to this logical error requires some genuine reflection. We have to ask: Is this an effect of the drug or an effect of the laws?

Confusing Metabolites with Intoxication

A single dose of marijuana does not create a 14-day high. I recently spoke before state representatives on a committee examining marijuana laws. One representative had learned that marijuana "stays in your system for weeks" and expressed concern that someone who used the drug over the weekend would create havoc on the road come Monday morning.

Marijuana metabolites remain detectable in the urine for extended periods. One of the best studies on the topic estimates that detectable levels of marijuana metabolites remain for two weeks after a single dose. A few people apparently think that these results mean that users remain high for 14 days after a single dose. Others have learned (correctly) that THC metabolites store in fat but think (incorrectly) that THC will somehow leak from fat cells at inopportune times and recreate intoxication. Uninformed citizens often assume that marijuana users will suddenly grow giddy or confused in the middle of landing an airplane or driving a forklift despite days of abstinence from the drug.

Nothing could be further from the truth. Most users report psychoactive effects that last a few hours. There seem to be no hangover effects the morning after use, much less any psychoactive effect days later. The urine screens frequently employed to detect marijuana can only reveal if the person has used the drug recently; they say nothing about current intoxication. A person who uses marijuana a few hours before the sample is taken can test negative because metabolites have yet to form. In contrast, a person who hasn't used marijuana in days and is experiencing no subjective effects can test positive because of marijuana consumption the week before. (A better alternative would be to test for current impairment for any reason rather than the presence of drugs.) Prohibitionists, anti-prohibitionists, and established scientists have made this error. This notion that metabolites remain for weeks appears in prohibitionist arguments, but the arguments often imply that intoxication or some sort of impairment lasts for weeks as well.

Anti-prohibitionists can unknowingly refer to research that makes this same error. For example, epidemiological studies suggest that marijuana use has no effect on traffic accidents, but these data rely on urine screens after accidents. The urine screens could have been negative even if the person was high at the time of the accident.

The Mental Filter

Strong attitudes can alter our perceptions of reality to the extent where we can't absorb information that counters the attitude. We simply see the world differently depending on what we think. Years ago I asked a large group of folks to define words like "shot," "spirits," and "toast." Heavy drinkers explained that a shot is an ounce and a half of booze, spirits are liquor, and a toast is the clinking of glasses before drinking. Light drinkers said that a shot is an injection of medicine from the doctor, spirits are ghosts, and toast is browned bread. People defined the words in ways that were consistent with their experience.

Prohibitionists and anti-prohibitionists can suffer from comparable filters. Compelling data appear to have little effect on prohibitionist attitudes about medical marijuana, for example. The last 3 drug czars have denied any medical use for marijuana, despite contrary conclusions by prestigious others, including the Institute of Medicine (1999). Reformers often minimize data on the potential for problems. In their zeal to end punishment, they seem to ignore the few who use the plant problematically. It's as if the data don't pass through their mental filter.

The cure for this problem may require more effort than the others. As we examine new data and new ideas, we have to ask ourselves to pay particular attention to those that contradict our own ideas. We have to be as critical of research that supports our ideas as we are of research that opposes it.

Kitchen Sinking

Many policy debates fly past each other. Folks on one side mention a specific point. Folks on the other side fail to address the point, and instead go into great detail about some other issue. Marital therapists call this "kitchen sinking"; they often see distressed couples yell back and forth at each other without sticking to a single issue, throwing everything, including the kitchen sink, at each other.

"You left your socks on the floor again!"

"Well, your mother can't stop criticizing me."

Note how these two sentences have nothing to do with each other. Policy debates often fall into the same trap.

"More than 700,000 Americans were arrested for marijuana last year!"

"Marijuana smokers report more coughs and bronchitis!"

Note how the second sentence is unrelated to the first. This is not a debate, but a collection of facts from each side. Rather than focus on a single topic, such as arrests or respiratory problems, folks bring out whatever comes to mind and spew it. Part of the problem arises from the needs of the news media. Debaters often have only a few seconds to speak. They have to get their most powerful argument out in a hurry. They can't follow a single train of thought in detail because they have to finish before the next commercial.

The cure for this problem is simple: Argue one point at a time. Although policy issues form a tangled web of implications and outcomes, we can do a much better job and come to rational conclusions by focusing on one issue before we move to the next.

The Cure

The way to avoid these errors and the depression associated with them requires a few simple steps. First and foremost, we have to identify them in our own arguments and those of others. Once we have a taxonomy of errors like this one, it's easier to recognize them. Few things are more frustrating than knowing an argument is wrong but being unable to identify what, exactly, is wrong with it. Naming these errors may help.

More Funding Is Needed for the War on Drugs

John P. Walters, interviewed by Advertising Age

John P. Walters is the director of the White House Office of National Drug Control Policy, the federal government agency that prosecutes the war on drugs in the United States. In the following 2006 interview with Advertising Age, *Walters discusses the effectiveness of using advertising campaigns to persuade young Americans against using drugs, especially marijuana. Walters urges Congress to approve $120 million in funding for the advertising program so that the agency can continue to make progress in reducing drug abuse.*

Advertising Age: *John P. Walters, director of the White House Office of National Drug Control Policy and the nation's drug czar, was initially dubious of the youth ad campaign, even threatening to end it, but has become a strong supporter.*

Is the drug campaign working?

John P. Walters: We've had a 19% decline [in drug use] and the President set of goal of 25% [drop by 2007] and while we are on track for that, we're still working to get as low or below what it was in 1992. . . . Do I expect it to go to zero? No. But I do not believe there's any inherent reason why this can't get to below the level of drug use we saw by teens and adults in 1992. We are not there.

How big should the campaign be?

Next year it should be $120 million. That's what we asked for.

Would more spending significantly affect results?

We have asked for consistently more money than Congress has given us. I think [denying us more] is a fundamental mistake. . . . In order [for drug use] to continue to go down and in order to not reverse [progress so far] we need to keep pressure on.

Why was more of a focus put on marijuana?

Of 60% [of drug abusers] over age 12 that need treatment, 7 million individuals, are dependent on marijuana. It's the single biggest cause of treatment need among illegal drugs, more than twice as important as the next biggest factor, cocaine. Of that 7 million, 23% are teenagers and we had intake data from the treatment systems indicating more teenagers were seeking treatment for marijuana than for all other illegal drugs combined. And for the first time, more than for alcoholism, which was always more available.

Isn't drug use cyclical, going up and down?

It goes up when you take your eye off the ball. I think the current of cultural self-abuse is an excuse made up by people who don't want to take responsibility for the children who are our responsibility now and will be next year. . . . If you are giving them healthy messages, they are healthier. If you encourage them to self-destruction, they are more self-destructive.

Is it realistic to expect advertising to completely deal with the issues or reasons people use drugs?

Can advertising be a substitute for all other things that come to play on young people and adults? No. Is advertising an enormously powerful contributing factor in people's choices and behavior? There is no question about that. Otherwise companies, politicians and we wouldn't advertise.

Have you seen any evidence that the campaign's focus on marijuana has affected its believability?

We know from the previous experience that there is a believability issue we have to be wary of. The exaggeration of dangers or threats can destroy the power or effectiveness of messaging. We haven't seen that. We have seen use go down.

If you had $120 million or more, would your job be easier? Could we be done with it?

If we got $120 million would [we] be able to do a better job? Yes. Would we waste money if we got more than that? No. But I wouldn't go so far as to say, that if you did X times 2, 3, 4 the campaign, drug use would go to virtually zero or halfway. There is a limit to how much we can get from this campaign alone.

But we are now below what I believe is an effective level. And I am very chagrined that despite the evidence of progress, despite the obvious history here, [drug use levels] can come back if you don't stay at it. We're about prevention. It is the smartest, the most cost-effective way to do this.

It's time for Congress to wake up and support a program that is working. We believe in accountability. We believe that programs that work ought to be funded. This program works like no other demand-reduction program in terms of the leverage results. There is no excuse for not supporting it except not paying attention.

The War on Drugs Should Not Include Marijuana

Silja J.A. Talvi

In the following article, Silja J.A. Talvi maintains that the White House Office of National Drug Control Policy (ONDCP) vastly distorts the significance of marijuana possession in the overall war on drugs in the United States. Perhaps more than being concerned about the drug itself, Talvi suggests, the ONDCP fears that the widespread normalization—or even the legalization—of marijuana use might lead to a decrease in political power and agency funding. As a result, Talvi argues, the federal government continues to promote the criminalization of marijuana use with an almost hysterical zeal, treating pot as a threat greater than alcohol, cocaine, and other hard drugs. According to Talvi such an extreme position has resulted in disproportionately unfair jail terms for those convicted of marijuana possession and in the unnecessary spending of billions of dollars on the campaign to keep marijuana illegal.

In a November 2002 letter to the nation's prosecutors, the White House's Office of National Drug Control Policy (ONDCP) didn't bother beating around the proverbial bush. "No drug matches the threat posed by marijuana," began the letter from Scott Burns, deputy director for state and local affairs.

The truth of the matter, as reiterated throughout that letter in terse language, was that marijuana was an addictive and dangerous drug linked to violent behavior on the part of users. To make matters worse, a subtle but powerful threat was identified as exacerbating the problem: well-financed and deceptive campaigns to normalize and ultimately legalize the use of marijuana.

Prosecutors were instructed to keep in mind the crucial importance of their role in fighting this threat of normalization in going after traffickers and dealers, and to tell the truth about marijuana to their communities: "The truth is that marijuana legalization would be a nightmare in America."

Yet these truths about marijuana hearken back to the absurdity of the *Reefer Madness* [a 1936 propaganda film about the dangers of marijuana] era of the 1930s, when marijuana use was linked to sexual promiscuity and violence, to say nothing of the imagined hordes of Mexicans and Blacks waiting to lure white women into pot-induced sinful acts.

Government Hysteria

Marijuana has been classified as a Schedule I drug since 1970, which means that for 35 long years, pot has been viewed by the federal government as a substance with no medicinal value and a high potential for abuse, more so than cocaine, for instance, which is a Schedule II drug. In many ways, modern-day government hysteria about the dangers of marijuana is far more distorted and far-fetched than the scare tactics that were employed under Harry J. Anslinger's reign [as commissioner from 1930 to 1962] at the Federal Bureau of Narcotics.

That's because we know a great deal more about marijuana today than we did in the '30s, particularly in the form of medical studies about the very real existence of cannabinoid receptors in human brains and the benefits of THC to chronic pain sufferers, as well as the fact that urban decriminalization results in neither more common nor more chronic use of marijuana.

As far as we've been able to trace it back, cannabis has been used by humans for at least 4,500 years. There has never been a single documented overdose from any form of consumption of the plant. (It's actually not technically possible for a human being to die from smoking marijuana, as Eric Schlosser points out in his book, *Reefer Madness*: a user would have to smoke 100 pounds a minute for 15 minutes to take a fatal dose.) On the other hand, people can and do die from drinking too much, smoking too much crack, shooting up unexpectedly pure heroin, and snorting or popping too much OxyContin.

With all of this knowledge available to the federal government, the extremist position of the ONDCP isn't just nonsensical, it actually sounds more and more like the product of truly paranoid, delusional thinking.

Whatever the reasons behind this kind of thinking, we do know that the ONDCP and successive presidential administrations since [Richard] Nixon's reign have been deadly serious about supporting this agenda, leaving no room for debate, much less any form of dissent. The extreme extent to which pot (and pot smokers) have been criminalized over the last few decades has had the effect of skewing what marijuana really is and isn't capable of doing to a person.

Assessing the Government's Drug Policy

That's something that any of the roughly 30,000 prisoners doing time for marijuana-related charges can surely attest to, as documented by the report, *Efficacy and Impact: The Criminal Justice Response to Marijuana Policy in the U.S.*, released last month [August 2005] from the Justice Policy Institute [JPI]. Thirty thousand may not seem like a hell of a lot when we've got 2.1 million folks behind bars from coast to coast, but that's 10,000 more people than the far more pot-friendly Netherlands has in its entire prison system.

According to that report, the U.S. drug control budget grew from $65 million in 1969 to nearly $19.2 *billion* in 2003, and we are now spending nearly 300 times more on drug control than just 35 years ago. Much of that money has been poured into law enforcement and incarceration, but a significant chunk of the ONDCP's funding has also gone toward media advertising, to the tune of $4.2 billion since 1997. According to research cited in the JPI report, most of those advertising dollars went toward anti-marijuana advertisements.

Marijuana, it would seem, is simply one of the greatest threats facing our nation.

Not so, says an increasingly vocal movement of marijuana and drug law reformists hailing from all over the political spectrum. Although there will always be the kinds of pot-worshipers who maintain that the Green Goddess can do no wrong, the message of this movement isn't that smoking cannabis is entirely without potential health risks. Moderate to heavy smokers do, in fact, run the risk of lung cancer or aggravating existing problems with depression or anxiety, among other potential problems. And absolutely no one is saying that marijuana is good for kids. Most parents would rather that their children stayed free and clear of (legal and illegal) drugs in general.

Pot Smoking Among Kids on the Rise

The thing is that the marijuana war doesn't seem to be doing a thing for keeping kids from smoking pot. In their *Efficacy and Impact* report, the JPI cites the Monitoring the Future Survey, an annual survey of 50,000 students from grades 8, 10 and 12. The recent survey actually found a 90 percent increase in the number of 8th graders who had tried pot, a 66 percent increase for 10th graders, and a 44 percent increase for seniors in high school. Thirteen years of increased marijuana arrests actually correspond to increased pot smoking by kids.

In other words, thousands of pot arrests and scare tactic messaging isn't doing anything to keep these kids from trying marijuana. It can be argued, on the contrary, that this drug war strategy is having an entirely detrimental effect.

Several research studies published in recent months have highlighted this and the many other highly flawed aspects of the war on marijuana. One of these, released in May 2005 by

The Sentencing Project, is about the 1990s transformation of the drug war into a war on marijuana.

Pointing to the fact that marijuana-related arrests added up to nearly half of 1.5 million drug-related arrests annually, the authors of this report noted that marijuana arrests actually increased by 113 percent between 1990 and 2002, while overall arrests in the nation decreased by 3 percent.

Who's Really Serving Time?

By way of spin control, the ONDCP has gone out of its way to say that the people being locked up are the real criminals: the money-making dealers and traffickers who operate in one of the nation's biggest and most lucrative underground economies.

The Sentencing Project's research refuted this easily. Of the marijuana arrests in 2002, nearly 9 in 10 were for possession, not dealing or trafficking. In addition, traffickers and dealers were actually getting shorter prison terms than those sentenced on possession charges: People sentenced for trafficking received a median of 9 months in prison, while those sentenced for possession received a median of 16 months in prison.

How's that for a head-scratcher?

The Cost of Waging the War on Drugs

From a fiscal standpoint, the bottom line has long since ceased making sense, as highlighted in Harvard economist Jeffrey Miron's academic paper in June 2005, *Budgetary Implications of Marijuana Prohibition.*

Through his research, Miron concluded that the annual cost of marijuana criminalization came in at a shocking $5.1 billion in 2000. Replacing the current criminalization model with one of taxation and regulation (not unlike that used for alcohol), he projected, would produce combined savings and tax revenues of $10–14 billion per year. The report, in turn, led more than 500 economists (led by Nobel prize winner Milton Friedman) to sign their names to an open letter to President [George W.] Bush calling for "an open and honest debate about marijuana prohibition that, would likely end up favoring a system where marijuana is legal but taxed and regulated like other goods."

Studies like Miron's aren't romanticizing or glamorizing cannabis consumption, and they're certainly not spurred on by hemp-and-pot-loving hippies pushing for world peace through THC [tetrahydrocannabinol, the main active chemical in marijuana].

Miron, Friedman and the other 500 economists were not taking a stand *for* pot, but rather against criminalization. This is a wholly different and more informed kind of public opposition than we've seen in recent decades. According to these studies, the War on Marijuana amounts to nothing more than an escalation of the fiscally irresponsible War on Drugs that bleeds state and federal coffers dry while ruining the lives of individuals and families in the process.

Drug Warriors Are in Denial

But this isn't the kind of truth that the ONDCP is interested in hearing—it's both inconvenient and embarrassing. Better just to ignore it altogether, right?

Vancouver Mayor Larry Campbell, a Royal Canadian Mounted Police constable, drug squad officer and chief British Columbia coroner who witnessed the height of mid-1990s drug overdose deaths (from heroin in particular), has himself become a proponent of both the decriminalization and eventual legalization of marijuana. Campbell resides across the border from one the U.S. counties that has seen the greatest increase in pot-related arrests. (King County, which includes the Greater Seattle Area, experienced a 418 percent growth rate in marijuana arrests from 1990 to 2002.)

In an interview with *Seattle Post-Intelligencer* columnist Joel Connelly, Mayor Campbell put it as matter-of-frankly as possible: "Drug czars are the most ill-informed people in government . . . [John Walters] is pushing an agenda that doesn't fit in the real world. He's in denial."

He's right, and the U.S. war on marijuana (and on illicit substances in general) is an abject failure. The emperor is wearing no clothes whatsoever; we should be willing to call his bluff.

Government Findings Underscore Marijuana Threat

U.S. Drug Enforcement Administration

The U.S. Drug Enforcement Administration (DEA) is the federal agency that enforces the controlled substances laws and regulations of the United States. Major objectives of the agency include the prevention of the illicit growth, manufacture, and distribution of drugs both domestically and internationally and the support of nonenforcement programs designed to reduce the accessibility of illegal substances. The following paper presents the DEA's official position on marijuana. The report states that there is no consensus among medical researchers that smoking marijuana provides relief to patients afflicted with chronic pain and certain diseases. However, the paper does highlight the harm that marijuana can cause abusers, including dependency, introduction to harder drugs, mental and physical health problems, increased delinquency, and impaired driving. The report argues that federal anti-marijuana programs are taking hold, observing that a recent Monitoring the Future *survey shows substantial decreases in marijuana use in the United States from 2001 to 2005. Further, the DEA's Domestic Cannabis Eradication/ Suppression program has overseen the destruction of more than 3 million plants in America's top seven marijuana-cultivating states.*

The campaign to legitimize what is called "medical" marijuana is based on two propositions: that science views marijuana as medicine, and that DEA [Drug Enforcement Administration] targets sick and dying people using the drug. Neither proposition is true. Smoked marijuana has not withstood the rigors of science—it is not medicine and it is not safe. DEA targets criminals engaged in cultivation and traf-

U.S. Drug Enforcement Administration, "The DEA Position on Marijuana," May 2006.

ficking, not the sick and dying. No state has legalized the trafficking of marijuana, including the twelve states that have decriminalized certain marijuana use.

Smoked Marijuana Is Not Medicine

There is no consensus of medical evidence that smoking marijuana helps patients. Congress enacted laws against marijuana in 1970 based in part on its conclusion that marijuana has no scientifically proven medical value. The Food and Drug Administration (FDA) is the federal agency responsible for approving drugs as safe and effective medicine based on valid scientific data. FDA has not approved smoked marijuana for any condition or disease. The FDA noted that "there is currently sound evidence that smoked marijuana is harmful," and "that no sound scientific studies supported medical use of marijuana for treatment in the United States, and no animal or human data supported the safety or efficacy of marijuana for general medical use."

In 2001, the Supreme Court affirmed Congress's 1970 judgment about marijuana in *United States v. Oakland Cannabis Buyers' Cooperative et al.* (2001), which held that, given the absence of medical usefulness, medical necessity is not a defense to marijuana prosecution. Furthermore, in *Gonzales v. Raich* (2005), the Supreme Court reaffirmed that the authority of Congress to regulate the use of potentially harmful substances through the federal Controlled Substances Act includes the authority to regulate marijuana of a purely intrastate character, regardless of a state law purporting to authorize "medical" use of marijuana.

The DEA and the federal government are not alone in viewing smoked marijuana as having no documented medical value. Voices in the medical community likewise do not accept smoked marijuana as medicine:

- The American Medical Association has rejected pleas to endorse marijuana as medicine, and instead has urged that marijuana remain a prohibited, Schedule I controlled substance, at least until more research is done.

- The American Cancer Society "does not advocate inhaling smoke, nor the legalization of marijuana," although the organization does support carefully controlled clinical studies for alternative delivery methods, specifically a THC [Tetrahydrocannabinol, the active ingredient in marijuana] skin patch.

- The American Academy of Pediatrics (AAP) believes that "[a]ny change in the legal status of marijuana, even if limited to adults, could affect the prevalence of use among adolescents." While it supports scientific research on the possible medical use of cannabinoids as opposed to smoked marijuana, it opposes the legalization of marijuana.

- The National Multiple Sclerosis Society (NMSS) states that studies done to date "have not provided convincing evidence that marijuana benefits people with MS [multiple selerosis]," and thus marijuana is not a recommended treatment. Furthermore, the NMSS warns that the "long-term use of marijuana may be associated with significant serious side effects."

- The British Medical Association (BMA) voiced extreme concern that down-grading the criminal status of marijuana would "mislead" the public into believing that the drug is safe. The BMA maintains that marijuana "has been linked to greater risk of heart disease, lung cancer, bronchitis and emphysema." The 2004 Deputy Chairman of the BMA's Board of Science said that "[t]he public must be made aware of the harmful effects we know result from smoking this drug."

- The American Academy of Pediatrics asserted that with regard to marijuana use, "from a public health perspective, even a small increase in use, whether attributable to increased availability or decreased perception of risk, would have significant ramifications."

In 1999, The Institute of Medicine (IOM) released a landmark study reviewing the supposed medical properties of marijuana. The study is frequently cited by "medical" marijuana advocates, but in fact severely undermines their arguments.

- After release of the IOM study, the principal investigators cautioned that the active compounds in marijuana may have medicinal potential and therefore should be researched further. However, the study concluded that "there is little future in smoked marijuana as a medically approved medication."

- For some ailments, the IOM found ". . . potential therapeutic value of cannabinoid drugs, primarily THC, for pain relief, control of nausea and vomiting, and appetite stimulation." However, it pointed out that "[t]he effects of cannabinoids on the symptoms studied are generally modest, and in most cases there are more effective medications [than smoked marijuana]."

- The study concluded that, at best, there is only anecdotal information on the medical benefits of smoked marijuana for some ailments, such as muscle spasticity. For other ailments, such as epilepsy and glaucoma, the study found no evidence of medical value and did not endorse further research.

- The IOM study explained that "smoked marijuana . . . is a crude THC delivery system that also delivers harmful substances." In addition, "plants contain a variable mixture of biologically active compounds and cannot be expected to provide a precisely defined drug effect." Therefore, the study concluded that "there is little future in smoked marijuana as a medically approved medication."

- The principal investigators explicitly stated that using smoked marijuana in clinical trials "should not be designed to develop it as a licensed drug, but should be a stepping stone to the development of new, safe delivery systems of cannabinoids."

Thus, even scientists and researchers who believe that certain active ingredients in marijuana may have potential medicinal value openly discount the notion that smoked marijuana is or can become "medicine."

DEA has approved and will continue to approve research into whether THC has any medicinal use. As of May 8, 2006, DEA had registered every one of the 163 researchers who requested to use marijuana in studies and who met Department of Health and Human Services standards. One of those researchers, The Center for Medicinal Cannabis Research (CMCR), conducts studies "to ascertain the general medical safety and efficacy of cannabis and cannabis products and examine alternative forms of cannabis administration." The CMCR currently has 11 on-going studies involving marijuana and the efficacy of cannabis and cannabis compounds as they relate to medical conditions such as HIV, cancer pain, MS, and nausea.

At present, however, the clear weight of the evidence is that smoked marijuana is harmful. No matter what medical condition has been studied, other drugs already approved by the FDA, such as Marinol—a pill form of synthetic THC—have been proven to be safer and more effective than smoked marijuana.

Marijuana Is Dangerous to the User and Others

Legalization of marijuana, no matter how it begins, will come at the expense of our children and public safety. It will create dependency and treatment issues, and open the door to use of other drugs, impaired health, delinquent behavior, and drugged drivers.

This is not the marijuana of the 1970's; today's marijuana is far more powerful. Average THC levels of seized marijuana rose from less than one per cent in the mid-1970's to a national average of over eight per cent in 2004. And the potency of "B.C. Bud" is roughly twice the national average—ranging from 15 per cent to as high as 25 per cent THC content.

Dependency and Treatment:

- Adolescents are at highest risk for marijuana addiction, as they are "three times more likely than adults to develop dependency." This is borne out by the fact that treatment admission rates for adolescents reporting marijuana as the primary substance of abuse increased from 32 to 65 per cent between 1993 and 2003. More young people ages 12–17 entered treatment in 2003 for marijuana dependency than for alcohol and all other illegal drugs combined.

- "[R]esearch shows that use of [marijuana] can lead to dependence. Some heavy users of marijuana develop withdrawal symptoms when they have not used the drug for a period of time. Marijuana use, in fact, is often associated with behavior that meets the criteria for substance dependence established by the American Psychiatric Association."

- Of the 19.1 million Americans aged 12 or older who used illicit drugs in the past 30 days in 2004, 14.6 million used marijuana, making it the most commonly used illicit drug in 2004.

- Among all ages, marijuana was the most common illicit drug responsible for treatment admissions in 2003, accounting for 15 per cent of all admissions—outdistancing heroin, the next most prevalent cause.

- In 2003, 20 per cent (185,239) of the 919,833 adults admitted to treatment for illegal drug abuse cited marijuana as their primary drug of abuse.

Marijuana as a Precursor to Abuse of Other Drugs:

- Marijuana is a frequent precursor to the use of more dangerous drugs, and signals a significantly enhanced likelihood of drug problems in adult life. The *Journal of the American Medical Association* reported, based on a study of 300 sets of twins, "that marijuana-using twins were four times more likely than their siblings to use cocaine and crack cocaine, and five times more likely to use hallucinogens such as LSD."

- Long-term studies on patterns of drug usage among young people show that very few of them use other drugs without first starting with marijuana. For example, one study found that among adults (age 26 and older) who had used cocaine, 62 per cent had initiated marijuana use before age 15. By contrast, less than one per cent of adults who never tried marijuana went on to use cocaine.

- Columbia University's National Center on Addiction and Substance Abuse reports that teens who used marijuana at least once in the last month are 13 times likelier than other teens to use another drug like cocaine, heroin, or methamphetamine, and almost 26 times likelier than those teens who have never used marijuana to use another drug.

- Marijuana use in early adolescence is particularly ominous. Adults who were early marijuana users were found to be five times more likely to become dependent on any drug, eight times more likely to use cocaine in the future, and fifteen times more likely to use heroin later in life.

- In 2003, 3.1 million Americans aged 12 or older used marijuana daily or almost daily in the past year. Of those daily marijuana users, nearly two-thirds "used at least one other illicit drug in the past 12 months." More than half (53.3 per cent) of daily marijuana users were also dependent on or abused alcohol or another illicit drug compared to those who were nonusers or used marijuana less than daily.

- Healthcare workers, legal counsel, police and judges indicate that marijuana is a typical precursor to meth-amphetamine. For instance, Nancy Kneeland, a substance abuse counselor in Idaho, pointed out that "in almost all cases meth users began with alcohol and pot."

Mental and Physical Health Issues Related to Marijuana:

- John Walters, Director of the Office of National Drug Control Policy, Charles G. Curie, Administrator of the Substance Abuse and Mental Health Services Administration, and experts and scientists from leading mental health organizations joined together in May 2005 to warn parents about the mental health dangers marijuana poses to teens. According to several recent studies, marijuana use has been linked with depression and suicidal thoughts, in addition to schizophrenia. These studies report that weekly marijuana use among teens doubles the risk of developing depression and triples the incidence of suicidal thoughts.

- Dr. Andrew Campbell, a member of the New South Wales (Australia) Mental Health Review Tribunal, published a study in 2005 which revealed that four out of five individuals with schizophrenia were regular cannabis users when they were teenagers. Between 75–80 per cent of the patients involved in the study used cannabis habitually between the ages of 12 and 21. In addition, a laboratory-controlled study by Yale scientists, published in 2004, found that THC "transiently induced a range of schizophrenia-like effects in healthy people."

- Smoked marijuana has also been associated with an increased risk of the same respiratory symptoms as tobacco, including coughing, phlegm production, chronic bronchitis, shortness of breath and wheezing. Because cannabis plants are contaminated with a range of fungal spores, smoking marijuana may also increase the risk of respiratory exposure by infectious organisms (i.e., molds and fungi).

- Marijuana takes the risks of tobacco and raises them: marijuana smoke contains more than 400 chemicals and increases the risk of serious health consequences, including lung damage.

- According to two studies, marijuana use narrows arteries in the brain, "similar to patients with high blood pressure and dementia," and may explain why memory tests are difficult for marijuana users. In addition, "chronic consumers of cannabis lose molecules called CB1 receptors in the brain's arteries," leading to blood flow problems in the brain which can cause memory loss, attention deficits, and impaired learning ability.

- Carleton University researchers published a study in 2005 showing that current marijuana users who smoke at least five "joints" per week did significantly worse than non-users when tested on neurocognition tests such as processing speed, memory, and overall IQ.

Delinquent Behaviors and Drugged Driving:

- In 2002, the percentage of young people engaging in delinquent behaviors "rose with [the] increasing frequency of marijuana use." For example, according to a National Survey on Drug Use and Health (NSDUH) report, 42.2 per cent of youths who smoked marijuana 300 or more days per year and 37.1 per cent of those who did so 50–99 days took part in serious fighting at school or work. Only 18.2 per cent of those who did not use marijuana in the past year engaged in serious fighting.

- A large shock trauma unit conducting an ongoing study found that 17 per cent (one in six) of crash victims tested positive for marijuana. The rates were slightly higher for crash victims under the age of eighteen, 19 per cent of whom tested positive for marijuana.

- In a study of high school classes in 2000 and 2001, about 28,000 seniors each year admitted that they were in at least one accident after using marijuana.

- Approximately 15 per cent of teens reported driving under the influence of marijuana. This is almost equal to the percentage of teens who reported driving under the influence of alcohol (16 per cent).

- A study of motorists pulled over for reckless driving showed that, among those who were not impaired by alcohol, 45 per cent tested positive for marijuana.

- The National Highway Traffic Safety Administration (NHTSA) has found that marijuana significantly impairs one's ability to safely operate a motor vehicle. According to its report, "[e]pidemiology data from road traffic arrests and fatalities indicate that after alcohol, marijuana is the most frequently detected psychoactive substance among driving populations." Problems reported include: decreased car handling performance, inability to maintain headway, impaired time and distance estimation, increased reaction times, sleepiness, lack of motor coordination, and impaired sustained vigilance.

Some of the consequences of marijuana-impaired driving are startling:

- The driver of a charter bus, whose 1999 accident resulted in the death of 22 people, had been fired from bus companies in 1989 and 1996 because he tested positive for marijuana four times. A federal investigator confirmed a report that the driver "tested positive for marijuana when he was hospitalized Sunday after the bus veered off a highway and plunged into an embankment."

- In April 2002, four children and the driver of a van died when the van hit a concrete bridge abutment after veering off the freeway. Investigators reported that the children nicknamed the driver "Smokey" because he regularly smoked marijuana. The driver was found at the crash scene with marijuana in his pocket.

- A former nurse's aide was convicted in 2003 of murder and sentenced to 50 years in prison for hitting a homeless man with her car and driving home with his mangled body "lodged in the windshield." The incident happened after a night of drinking and taking drugs, including marijuana. After arriving home, the woman parked her car, with the man still lodged in the windshield, and left him there until he died.

- In April 2005, an eight year-old boy was killed when he was run over by an unlicensed 16 year-old driver who police believed had been smoking marijuana just before the accident.

- In 2001, George Lynard was convicted of driving with marijuana in his bloodstream, causing a head-on collision that killed a 73 year-old man and a 69 year-old woman. Lynard appealed this conviction because he allegedly had a "valid prescription" for marijuana. A Nevada judge agreed with Lynard and granted him a new trial. The case has been appealed to the Nevada Supreme Court.

- Duane Baehler, 47, of Tulsa, Okalahoma was "involved in a fiery crash that killed his teenage son" in 2003. Police reported that Baehler had methamphetamine, cocaine and marijuana in his system at the time of the accident.

Marijuana also creates hazards that are not always predictable. In August 2004, two Philadelphia firefighters died battling a fire that started because of tangled wires and lamps used to grow marijuana in a basement closet.

Marijuana and Incarceration

Federal marijuana investigations and prosecutions usually involve hundreds of pounds of marijuana. Few defendants are incarcerated in federal prison for simple possession of marijuana.

- In 2001, there were 24,299 offenders sentenced in federal court on drug charges. Of those, only 2.3 per cent (186 people) were sentenced for simple possession. In addition, it is important to recognize that many inmates were initially charged with more serious crimes but negotiated reduced charges to simple possession through plea agreements.

- According to the latest survey data in a 2005 ONDCP [White House Office of National Drug Control Policy] study, marijuana accounted for 13 per cent of all state drug offenders in 1997, and of the inmates convicted of marijuana offenses, only 0.7 per cent were incarcerated for marijuana possession alone.

The Foreign Experience

The Netherlands:

- Due to international pressure on permissive Dutch cannabis policy and domestic complaints over the spread of marijuana "coffee shops," the government of the Netherlands has reconsidered its legalization measures. After marijuana became normalized, consumption nearly tripled—from 15 per cent to 44 per cent—among 18 to 20 year-old Dutch youth. As a result of stricter local government policies, the number of cannabis "coffeehouses" in the Netherlands was reduced—from 1,179 in 1997 to 737 in 2004, a 37 per cent decrease in 7 years.

- About 70 per cent of Dutch towns have a zero-tolerance policy toward cannabis cafes.

- In August 2004, after local governments began clamping down on cannabis "coffeehouses" seven years earlier, the government of the Netherlands formally announced a shift in its cannabis policy through the United National International Narcotics Control Board (INCB). According to "an inter-ministerial policy paper on cannabis, the government acknowledged that 'cannabis is not harmless'—neither for the abusers, nor for the community." Netherlands intends to reduce the number of coffee shops (especially those near border areas and schools), closely monitor drug tourism, and implement an action plan to discourage cannabis use.

This public policy change brings the Netherlands "closer towards full compliance with the international drug control treaties with regard to cannabis."

- Dr. Ernest Bunning, formerly with Holland's Ministry of Health and a principal proponent of that country's liberal drug philosophy, has acknowledged that, "[t]here are young people who abuse soft drugs ... particularly those that have [a] high THC [content]. The place that cannabis takes in their lives becomes so dominant they don't have space for the other important things in life. They crawl out of bed in the morning, grab a joint, don't work, smoke another joint. They don't know what to do with their lives."

Switzerland:

- Liberalization of marijuana laws in Switzerland has likewise produced damaging results. After liberalization, Switzerland became a magnet for drug users from many other countries. In 1987, Zurich permitted drug use and sales in a part of the city called Platzpitz, dubbed "Needle Park." By 1992, the number of regular drug users at the park reportedly swelled from a "few hundred at the outset in 1987 to about 20,000." The area around the park became crime-ridden, forcing closure of the park. The experiment has since been terminated.

Canada:

- After a large decline in the 1980s, marijuana use among teens increased during the 1990s as young people became "confused about the state of federal pot law" in the wake of an aggressive decriminalization campaign, according to a special adviser to Health Canada's Director General of drug strategy. Several Canadian drug surveys show that marijuana use among Canadian youth has steadily climbed to surpass its 26-year peak, rising to 29.6 per cent of youth in grades 7–12 in 2003.

United Kingdom:

- In March 2005, British Home Secretary Charles Clarke took the unprecedented step of calling "for a rethink on Labour's legal downgrading of cannabis" from a Class B to a Class C substance. Mr. Clarke requested that the Advisory Council on the Misuse of Drugs complete a new report, taking into account recent studies showing a link between cannabis and psychosis and also considering the more potent cannabis referred to as "skunk."

- In 2005, during a general election speech to concerned parents, British Prime Minister Tony Blair noted that medical evidence increasingly suggests that cannabis is not as harmless as people think and warned parents that young people who smoke cannabis could move on to harder drugs.

The Legalization Lobby

The proposition that smoked marijuana is "medicine" is, in sum, false—trickery used by those promoting wholesale legalization. When a statute dramatically reducing penalties for "medical" marijuana took effect in Maryland in October 2003, a defense attorney noted that "[t]here are a whole bunch of people who like marijuana who can now try to use this defense." The attorney observed that lawyers would be "neglecting their clients if they did not try to find out what 'physical, emotional or psychological'" condition could be enlisted to develop a defense to justify a defendant's using the drug. "Sometimes people are self-medicating without even realizing it," he said.

- Ed Rosenthal, senior editor of *High Times*, a pro-drug magazine, once revealed the legalizer strategy behind the "medical" marijuana movement. While addressing an effort to seek public sympathy for glaucoma patients, he said, "I have to tell you that I also use marijuana medically. I have a latent glaucoma which has never been diagnosed. The reason why it's never been diagnosed is because I've been treating it." He continued, "I have to be honest, there is another reason why I do use marijuana . . . and that is because I like to get high. Marijuana is fun."

- A few billionaires—not broad grassroots support— started and sustain the "medical" marijuana and drug legalization movements in the United States. Without their money and influence, the drug legalization movement would shrivel. According to National Families in Action, four individuals—George Soros, Peter Lewis, George Zimmer and John Sperling—contributed $1,510,000 to the effort to pass a "medical" marijuana law in California in 1996, a sum representing nearly 60 per cent of the total contributions.

- In 2000 the *New York Times* interviewed Ethan Nadelmann, Director of the Lindesmith Center. Responding to criticism that the medical marijuana issue is a stalking horse for drug legalization, Mr. Nadelmann stated: "Will it help lead toward marijuana legalization? . . . I hope so."

- In 2004, Alaska voters faced a ballot initiative that would have made it legal for adults age 21 and older to possess, grow, buy, or give away marijuana. The measure also called for state regulation and taxation of the drug. The campaign was funded almost entirely by the Washington, D.C.–based Marijuana Policy Project, which provided "almost all" the $857,000 taken in by the pro-marijuana campaign. Fortunately, Alaskan voters rejected the initiative.

- In October 2005, Denver voters passed Initiative 100 decriminalizing marijuana based on incomplete and misleading campaign advertisements put forth by the Safer Alternative For Enjoyable Recreation (SAFER). A Denver City Councilman complained that the group used the slogan "Make Denver SAFER" on billboards and campaign signs to mislead the voters into thinking that the initiative supported increased police staffing. Indeed, the Denver voters were never informed of the initiative's true intent to decriminalize marijuana.

- The legalization movement is not simply a harmless academic exercise. The mortal danger of thinking that marijuana is "medicine" was graphically illustrated by a story from California. In the spring of 2004, Irma Perez was "in the throes of her first experience with the drug ecstasy" when, after taking one ecstasy tablet, she became ill and told friends that she felt like she was "going to die." Two teenage acquaintances did not seek medical care and instead tried to get Perez to smoke marijuana. When that failed due to her seizures, the friends tried to force-feed marijuana leaves to her, "apparently because [they] knew that drug is sometimes used to treat cancer patients." Irma Perez lost consciousness and died a few days later when she was taken off life support. She was 14 years old.

Still, There's Good News

Continued Declines in Marijuana Use Among Youth

In 2005, the *Monitoring the Future (MTF)* survey recorded an overall 19.1 per cent decrease in current use of illegal drugs between 2001 and 2005, edging the nation closer to its five-year goal of a 25 per cent reduction in illicit drug use in 2006. Specific to marijuana, the 2005 MTF survey showed:

- Between 2001 and 2005, marijuana use dropped in all three categories: lifetime (13%), past year (15%) and 30-day use (19%). Current marijuana use decreased 28 per cent among 8th graders (from 9.2% to 6.6%), and 23 per cent among 10th graders (from 19.8% to 15.2%).

Increased Eradication

- As of September 20, 2005, DEA's Domestic Cannabis Eradication/Suppression Program supported the eradication of 3,054,336 plants in the top seven marijuana producing states (California, Hawaii, Kentucky, Oregon, Tennessee, Washington and West Virginia). This is an increase of 315,628 eradicated plants over the previous year.

- For the 2005 eradication season, a total of 5 million marijuana plants have been eradicated across the United States. This is a one million plant increase over last year. The Departments of Agriculture and Interior combined have eradicated an estimated 1.2 million plants during this 2005 eradication season.

CHAPTER 5

Personal Accounts of Growing and Smoking Marijuana

Spreading Marijuana Worldwide

Clifford Krauss

In the following article journalist Clifford Krauss provides an exposé on Canadian marijuana reform activist and entrepreneur, Marc Emery. Known as the "Prince of Pot" in Canada, Emery has been indicted by the U.S. federal government on charges of selling millions of dollars worth of marijuana seeds in several American states. Out on bail and residing in British Columbia where marijuana laws are relatively lenient, Emery vows to continue selling marijuana seeds all over the world until "it will be impossible for governments to eradicate or control" the plant.

Freshly released on bail, Marc Emery faced the camera of his Pot-TV.net Web site the other day to make an urgent appeal for money to finance his legal struggle to avert extradition to the United States for trafficking marijuana seeds south of the border.

"Let me be the light that shines on the American gulag," he said, stern-eyed, pointing into the camera. Without notes, Mr. Emery sermonized for a half-hour about everything from the marvelous medicinal and spiritual qualities of pot to the greatness of Thomas Jefferson, "who gave America on hemp paper the Declaration of Independence."

"Marijuana made me a better parent, a better lover, a better businessman," he solemnly told his supporters. Immediately after the broadcast, he was quick to add, "a better driver, too."

The Prince of Pot

At 47, Mr. Emery is known as the Prince of Pot, even in his recent federal indictment in Seattle for charges of conspiring to manufacture marijuana, launder money and traffic millions of marijuana seeds into the United States. At the time of his arrest, on July 29 [2005], he and his business were on a United States attorney general list of the 46 most wanted international drug traffickers, and the only one in Canada. But his clownish nickname provides a clue that Mr. Emery is not your typical drug kingpin from the movies who deals in the shadows.

A lanky Canadian with a taste for bland T-shirts and chinos, he proudly promotes himself as the leader of the sizable Vancouver marijuana counterculture that is condoned by the municipal government and much of the city's population. He postures as just a regular guy who loves the Vancouver Canucks, and rarely smokes more than a joint or two a day.

But he also freely says that, outside the Netherlands, he has sold more marijuana seeds and offered the largest selection of any seed bank in the world. He adds that the amount of seeds he has sold south of the border "qualifies me for the death penalty in the United States." (The first claim, of ubiquity, is accepted by American prosecutors, while the second, of a looming death sentence, is met with guffaws.)

"I have a master plan," Mr. Emery said in an interview in the offices of his magazine, *Cannabis Culture.* "I've wanted to be the Johnny Appleseed of marijuana, so if we produced millions and millions of marijuana plants all over the world, it would be impossible for governments to eradicate or control all of it."

In other words, he added, he wants "to overgrow the governments" that punish marijuana users.

A Dedicated Marijuana Advocate and Entrepreneur

In his crusade to make marijuana completely legal everywhere, not just in Canada, where anti-pot laws are already more lenient than in the United States, Mr. Emery has marketed his seeds and anti-prohibition message on his Web site and magazine and traveled around the country smoking marijuana in front of police stations.

As leader of the British Columbia Marijuana Party, he has run candidates across the province and has himself run for mayor twice in Vancouver on the platform of disbanding the police force and remaking it from scratch. Armed with a speaking style that resembles a tommy gun firing off sound bites, he came in a respectable fifth out of 16 candidates in the last mayoral election, in 2002.

To the growing annoyance of American law enforcement, he has been openly selling seeds to American growers and counseling them how best to cultivate his product and avoid the attention of the police—all with only minor harassment, until now, from Canadian law enforcement.

According to the United States Drug Enforcement Administration [DEA], Mr. Emery has sold millions of dollars worth of seeds to growers in California, Florida, Indiana, Michigan, Montana, New Jersey, North Dakota, Tennessee and Virginia.

"He operated his business very efficiently, making a lot of money at the expense of our kids and the American public," Rodney Benson, special agent in charge of the D.E.A. field division in Seattle, said in an interview.

Government Pressure Increases

Now, his master plan is in serious jeopardy. In July, the Canadian police, working with D.E.A. agents, arrested Mr. Emery and raided his headquarters at the request of the American government, so that he might be extradited for trial in Seattle. Last week [August 2005], he was freed on bail; the extradition process could take years. It is bound to stir a debate in Canada about whether it should permit a Canadian to stand trial in the United States for an offense that is essentially tolerated here [in Canada]. But for the time being, Mr. Emery's empire is in tatters. He has been forced to lay off workers at his magazine and Web site, and because he can no longer sell seeds, his ability to finance marijuana-legalization causes has dried up. He says he must move to a smaller apartment, give up his car lease and live on the equivalent of $32 a day from donations.

"Lets face it," Mr. Emery said in an interview. "I've sold millions of seeds and I've been doing it every day of my life the last 11 years. I'm so transparent that everyone from the prime minister to the guy on the street knows it."

He says he has made $4 million in profit since 1996 selling seeds in his Vancouver store, by mail and on the Internet. But he says he has not saved a dime, does not own a share of stock or bonds, does not even own a piece of property.

Investing in Marijuana Reform

All the money he has made, he says, has gone into his magazine, his Internet Pot-TV news channel, his British Columbia Marijuana Party, various referendum initiatives for marijuana legalization in the United States, legal fees for marijuana growers in several countries and support for his wife, various ex-lovers and four adopted children.

He also claims to have paid nearly $600,000 in taxes from the proceeds of his seeds, noting openly on his tax returns that he worked as a vendor of marijuana seeds.

Mr. Emery describes himself as "a responsible libertarian, not a hedonist," who extols the virtues of capitalism, low taxes, small government and the right of citizens to bear arms.

He said he grew up a social democrat, influenced by his father, who was active in trade union work. But he said his life changed in 1979 when he began reading the works of Ayn Rand, who championed individual freedom and capitalism.

"The right to be free, the right to own the fruits of your mind and effort now all made sense," he recalled. Only a few months after discovering Rand, his girlfriend at the time offered him a joint and he smoked marijuana for the first time.

A Committed Libertarian

"It was an epiphany," he said. "I had a sixth sense added to my five senses. The silence sounded different, smells were more nuanced and the brightness of the moon made it look bigger and more substantial in the sky."

The combination of Rand's philosophy and the marijuana set him on a course of advocacy in which, he said, "I decided to dedicate my whole life to repudiate the state."

Then living in London, Ontario, he sold banned marijuana and pornography books and magazines, contested laws limiting the right of stores to open on Sundays and led a municipal tax revolt. He even resisted a municipal garbage strike, by renting a truck and picking up the garbage himself.

After traveling for a while in Asia, however, he has dedicated his efforts to promoting marijuana and its culture.

"Now the Goliath, now the evil empire has made its move on me," Mr. Emery told his Web site audience. But he promised that his crusade would continue "till liberty or till death."

Parents Consider the Pros and Cons of Continuing to Smoke Pot

Larry Smith

*A professed recreational user of marijuana, Larry Smith consid-
ers how members of his generation who are becoming parents
should broach the subject of drug use with their children. Smith
observes that while some parents choose to give up smoking pot
altogether when they have kids, others continue to enjoy the
drug responsibly. Whether or not parents still smoke marijuana,
Smith contends, they face the dilemma of talking to their kids
about drugs without being viewed as hypocritical. As Smith dis-
covers, parents have strikingly different opinions about how to
handle the matter: Some declare that they will be honest with
their children, while others admit that they will tell an outright
lie about their own past drug use. Still other parents indicate
that they will level with their children on a need-to-know basis,
educating their kids about the pros and cons of marijuana use
without revealing the sordid details of their own personal experiences with drugs.*

How do you tell your kids to stay away from drugs when
you used to do them, or—gasp—still do? What if you
don't think drugs are so very wrong?

Twelve years ago, back when you could put things in the
mail without a return address, my old college buddy Jim sent
me a package. Opening the plain, brown box, I was surprised
at its contents: the small purple bong he and I had put to very
good use in the late '80s and early '90s. Along with this stained
relic he had scribbled a note of explanation: "Getting married

and planning to have children, so I guess I won't be needing this anymore." I wasn't sure what unnerved me more: his decision that "growing up" meant giving up something that he enjoyed without incident, or the implied idea that I was stuck in a hazy past while he moved on to an appropriate, adult future.

The second time I experienced In Loco Bongus I thought: This is getting weird (and also: What am I going to do with two bongs?). This time my co-worker walked into my office, closed the door, and sheepishly explained that while he and his glass two-footer had had some great times together, his son was getting older, he had a second on the way, and he didn't want anyone under 4 feet to stumble across it accidentally. "I don't want my boy to think it's OK to be a pothead," he explained. "Well, that's not true, I don't want him to think it's OK to be a full-blown hazed-out pothead." Which is why he switched to a much smaller, more easily stashed pipe.

According to the 2002 National Survey on Drug Use and Health, more than a third of Americans over the age of 12 have tried marijuana at some point in their life—that's 80 million people who actually admit it, and I suspect there are a couple more who don't. Many of these millions can look at their offspring with a straight face and explain that while they once experimented with drugs during the folly of their youth, now they don't—and neither should you, little man.

That must be nice for them. I don't know many of these people. The people I have spent the last decade working and playing with have inhaled more than a few puffs and taken a variety of trips down Alice's rabbit hole. Yet some way, somehow they have turned into able and impressive members of the republic.

These are people with good jobs, who engage in charitable pursuits and who rarely cut in line at Whole Foods. We've taken some of our old vices with us into adulthood without burning down the house or checking into rehab. We've done a good job prolonging our adolescence, but now we're facing adulthood's ultimate gut check: children.

And when it comes to kids, we have a drug problem.

What to tell the children about past—and, in many cases, current—drug use ain't easy. Should we practice what we preach?

Should we lie? Where do you draw the line between being a hypocrite and protecting your kids? Are we worse parents if we get high in front of our kids than if we have a couple of stiff drinks?

How do we reconcile our own experiences with drugs— ones that have been overwhelmingly positive—with the very real possibility that our kids could run into trouble with what are in fact potent substances?

Before you write nasty letters to the editor denouncing my friends and me for advocating drug use, let's be clear: Scores of people have had their lives and the lives of those around them destroyed by drugs.

No one I know believes that all drugs are good nor wishes a nation of junkies on anyone. Drugs are not for all people, all drugs are not for all drug users, and no illicit drugs are good for children.

Among my close friends, there's a general feeling that there are "good" drugs and "bad" drugs.

The good ones are empathetic and eye-opening (MDMA [Ecstacy], marijuana, hallucinogens). The bad ones are ego-driven and destructive (coke, speed, heroin). Both types can destroy you—it's just that they haven't in our case. In a topic that doesn't deal much in grays, this is a nuanced and certainly unpopular point of view. So it's no surprise, if a bit disappointing, that most of the people I talked to asked to have their names changed.

"I'm not nervous at all about talking to my sons about sex," says my friend Rob, a 32-year-old writer living in Brooklyn, N.Y., with his wife and two small boys, aged 1 and 5. "But

I'm scared shitless to talk to them about drugs." Rob smokes as much as two to three times a week, but never when his children are awake.

He thinks the worst thing for him to have heard when he was a kid would have been that smoking pot is acceptable. "I would have been off to the races," he says. That's why Rob is hesitant to be completely honest with his own children about his drug use. "I probably won't be fully open about my drug use until my sons are in their 20s, post-college maybe.

I feel like I have to give him guidance before that, but I'm not going to tell him about the time I dropped two hits of E [Ecstacy] and two tabs of acid and had my brain melt while I watched the Breeders and the Beastie Boys at Lollapalooza. I can't say, 'Make sure you don't melt your brain like daddy!'"

"My push for parents is always to be open and honest," says Marsha Rosenbaum, who leads workshops for parents on how to handle drug use among their kids as director of the Safety First project of the Drug Policy Alliance. "Kids have amazing bullshit detectors and are probably going to know that we aren't telling the truth. To the parents who stopped using drugs, I say tell them your story and tell them the real story."

Drug story hour's a tough one, but many of my friends want to tell their children about all of their experiences—the good and the bad and the hazy in betweens—eventually. Knowing whom to tell what when is the hard part. Rob says he knows exactly what he'll say to his kids when they're 25; he just has no idea what to tell them when they're 10.

"My husband and I won't hide our pot use from our daughter because it's just such a natural part of our lives," says Carla, a 35-year-old communications specialist in Oakland, Calif., and mother of an 8-month-old girl. "But while she's growing up will we tell her Mommy and Daddy loved having sex on coke in a hotel room when she was staying with Grandma? Will we tell a teenage girl that the occasional line of K [Ketamine] is a blast? Absolutely not. The important thing is to explain that drugs are for adults who are old enough to handle them, and that they will have a chance to experiment soon enough in life if that's what they want to do."

Allie, a 33-year-old legal aid attorney in Washington, D.C., who has been known to enjoy a large cocktail of substances over the years, is planning a family now and suspects she'll take a somewhat less tolerant—perhaps hypocritical—approach. "I won't tell them about my own use until they're old enough not to be influenced by it, which I think is 16 to 18 depending on the kid, because I won't tolerate any drug use from them," she says. "It just seems like they'll have so many sources in their lives justifying drug use—from friends to hormones to boredom to the Internet—that they will also need to have something on the other side balancing it."

I myself don't have kids. I may very well someday, and as I get older I can increasingly understand the temptation to just out and out lie to them about a variety of parts of my life, especially my drug use. I mean, do I really want to tell Larry Jr. that daddy had a mind-altering moment on mushrooms at Joshua Tree when he was 23, but my dear, my dear boy, if I ever find mushrooms in your backpack you'll be grounded from now until your freshman year in college?

"I would be much more concerned if my kids thought I was a hypocrite than if they thought I was a pothead," says my friend Alan, a professor of English at Indiana University and soon-to-be father of twins.

Alan's been thinking a lot about what he's going to tell his children about his daily pot use, a habit he suspects won't be so compatible with the daily rigors of daddyhood. "I'll tell them that I smoke, I like it, but that it's not for everyone," he says. "I will tell them that I did certain drugs for adventure and exploration, but never to counter self-esteem and an inability to tolerate reality. I will tell them if they decide to try drugs, I hope they tell me and I'll demand that they be safe."

Safe is actually less subjective than it may sound. "Just as you can't use a chain saw or drive until you are a certain age, you shouldn't use drugs until you are old enough to be able to handle it," says Mitch Earleywine, a professor at the University of Southern California and author of *Understanding Marijuana: A New Look at the Scientific Evidence.* Earleywine says new studies reveal that cannabis can interfere with the brain's development before the age of 17. It stands to reason that a compelling case can be made for telling your kids to hold off until after high school graduation, even if you didn't.

A current Office of National Drug Control Policy [ONDCP] anti-drug campaign seeks to help confused adults reconcile their past use with whatever version of "just say no" they're trying to work out as they raise kids. Called "Hypocrite," it reads: "So you smoke pot. And now your kid's trying it and you feel like you can't say anything. Get over it. Smoking pot can affect the brain and lead to other risky behaviors. So you have to set the rules and expect your kid to live drug free no matter how hypocritical it makes you feel."

"In the focus groups we asked parents to identify some of the barriers that existed in talking to kids about drugs—and their own experience with drugs came up as one of those barriers," says Jennifer DeVallance, a spokesperson for the ONDCP. "These ads are saying: You need to step up to the plate, regardless of what your experience was."

Unlike the folks in the government's focus group, most of my friends don't think their own past makes them hypocrites, but rather better informed parents. Jill, an interior designer who lives outside of Nashville, Tenn., with her teenage son, says that she's not so worried about her son's experimentation because she has so much experience with drugs herself. "If you never did drugs as a teen, or any other time in your life, I suspect all you can think about is your kid behaving like he or she is a character in *Reefer Madness* [a 1936 propaganda film about the dangers of marijuana] or that he's going to become Robert Downey Jr.," she says. Jill has resigned herself to the fact that her son does drugs, but she is tough with him about his use. "We talked about what some people can handle and others can't." She explained to him that in her mind, pot is on par with alcohol: Both get you high, both should be taken in moderation and both can have devastating effects on your life if you overindulge. "Once I knew about his use, I told him what I had done," she says. "Not everything all at once. I didn't want my former experiments to encourage him, and it was more information than he needed at one sitting."

"If you didn't think your drug use was a big mistake, don't tell them that it was a big mistake, which is what the government wants you to say," says Rosenbaum. "Tell them that they were probably attracted to it for the same reasons that you were. And if you quit, tell them why."

Delia, a 47-year-old physical therapist in Manhattan with a 13-year-old daughter, agrees. "I will tell her drugs were fun and seductive," she says, "but ultimately they were a mistake." Knowing that Delia had a pretty wild ride in the late '60s and '70s, I ask her if she plans to tell her daughter the whole story.

Her answer is an unflinching no. "I can't ever tell her everything I did, especially that I tried heroin," she says. "I tried it once and liked it so much that I knew it could destroy me. A survival instinct kicked in, one I don't know would kick in for her. But I can't tell her the entire truth of my use because I don't want to influence her."

And there's the riddle: There's no more influential person in a child's life than a parent.

Therefore, in one way or another, every parent I talked to felt that to a certain degree they had to lie to their kids about drugs. Yet almost in the same breath, few want to mask what for at least a certain period in their life was a very real, important and joyful part of who they were and are as people.

"My goal as a parent," says Carla, "is to give her the tools to know what she can handle and what's too much. I don't want her to say no to drugs, because they can be freakin' fun. It's not a popular perspective, but it's true. Fun is a big part of my life, and drugs are a part of fun."

"But you know what?" she says with a pregnant pause, "my perspective today could change a lot in 10 years."

If so, I fear I'll be getting another bong in the mail.

Getting High with My Children

Marni Jackson

Citing a recent report that some 1.5 million Canadian adults smoke marijuana recreationally, Marni Jackson reports on a segment of this group who think that it is okay to smoke pot with their children. Through interviews with both kids and parents, Jackson observes that parents who smoke marijuana with their children are often "baby boomers" who grew up in the 1960s era of drug experimentation and who are more tolerant of pot than hard drugs or binge drinking; further, these parents feel that if their kids are going to smoke pot anyway, they would rather have them do it in the safety of their own home. Those who oppose this practice, Jackson writes, argue that parents have a responsibility to act as positive role models for their children and to set limits that will teach them to make good choices as adults. Jackson also notes a number of parents and kids express concern about the potential dangers of smoking too much marijuana at a young age, citing negative mental and physical effects, the increased likelihood of dropping out of school, and addiction.

"It was a little weird, seeing my parents stoned," Tom confesses. The Toronto high school student was describing the first time he'd smoked marijuana—at home last spring, just after turning 17, when he shared a joint with his hard-working, middle-class parents. "But I had an amazing, fantastic connection with my dad, and it was a good experience for all of us. They showed me how to take the seeds and stems out of the pot. Then, basically, we ate. My mom ordered sushi, and we made a mountain of nachos. It kind of felt like a rite of passage."

Marni Jackson, "Pass the Weed, Dad," *Maclean's*, vol. 118, November 7, 2005. © 2005 by *Maclean's* Magazine. Reproduced by permission of the author.

After his family initiation, Tom bought six or seven joints of his own for a camping trip, "and that was cool too." But his new girlfriend didn't approve of pot, or him on it. "She said there was this separation thing that happened whenever I smoked." So Tom gave it up, even though his older sister had just given him a nice handmade pipe for his birthday. "But my other sister could care less about pot. Lots of kids try it and don't like it. I think it's totally individual."

Nicole, who maintained a scholarship throughout university and has now graduated, grew up in a household where pot smoking was as casually present as wine with dinner. "Marijuana was so integrated into our social life that it didn't seem to make sense to hide it," says her father, a lawyer. "So we didn't. She began smoking pot when she was around 16. This was in the nineties, when the police were pretty aggressive about it, so we thought that it was safer for her to smoke at home than in the streets. And then when she was in college, there were definitely times when she and I would smoke a joint together. Or I might buy some pot and give her some."

"But lately, we've made some new rules. No smoking dope together. No tobacco in the house. We are rethinking things in general."

He pauses. "Yes, we were open about smoking pot around her. But was it a good idea? I don't know."

Nicole, now 24, says she's "always believed it was a good thing that it wasn't hidden or taboo. I've seen a lot of sheltered kids who got into it at 12 or 13, as rebellion. I wasn't interested till later. I tried it and thought, 'Hey, this is good!' It was relaxing, and fun, and it numbs you out, which can be a good thing."

Boomer Parents Are Torn

Most parents, of course, aren't sitting around the family bong with their kids. They go along with the authorities who view marijuana as a drug with addictive potential that turns kids into over-snacking, under-motivated, learning-impaired couch potatoes. But the 1.5 million Canadian adults who, according to the Canadian Medical Association, smoke marijuana recreationally might not agree. In fact, a recent Canadian Addiction Survey found that 630,000 of us aged 15 and older smoke cannabis every day. And among middle-aged Canadians, dope use in the past year has increased from 1.4 per cent in 1994 to 8.4 per cent in 2004.

Perhaps as a consequence of this ongoing boomer buzz, some parents feel a zero-tolerance policy with teenagers simply doesn't work and may only increase the allure of pot. They would rather keep the lines of communication open, talk to their children about the genuine risks of individual drugs, and help them develop their own good judgment about drug use—whether it's tobacco, alcohol or marijuana.

Sharing a joint with your 16- or 17-year-old may be pushing it. Nevertheless, parents who talk about "drugs" as if they're all the same, equating pot with more lethal substances like cocaine or crystal meth—a popular form of amphetamine that is wildly addictive and blatantly destructive—run the risk of not being listened to at all. When we demonize drugs, ironically we tend to empower the drugs, rather than our kids.

Families have changed since the days of *Father Knows Best* (the equivalent show today would be "Father Tokes Best"). Many parents are veterans of the counterculture who did a lot more than inhale in the sixties. For some, marijuana was just an ambient phase, like black-light posters. Others have grown up into successful, civilized, recreational pot smokers who don't want to lie to their kids. They consider the moderate use of pot to be a relatively benign activity—and certainly better than drinking eight beers and getting behind the wheel of a car. Binge drinking, which has become epidemic among college students, can also be fatal, but no one has ever died from a marijuana overdose (although it carries its own health risks, affects driving ability, and has certainly caused repeated screenings of bad movies).

One thing is clear, though: regardless of whether their parents are strict or permissive, most kids will try cannabis sooner or later. By the time they exit their teen years, the Canadian Addiction Survey reports, 70 per cent of them will have smoked a joint at some point—if not in the past hour. Among everyone who's tried it, 18 per cent smoke daily.

Tom and Nicole waited longer than most teenagers to experiment with marijuana. The average age of first use has gone down, from 14.5 years in 1995 to 13.7 in 2003. In fact, Toronto's Centre for Addiction and Mental Health (CAMH) reports that five per cent of school kids have tried pot before the end of Grade 6. (Can the preschool doobie be far behind? Hemp soothers?) Twenty-eight per cent of students who've finished Grade 9 will have smoked pot in the past year. Roughly the same percentage, it's worth noting, have never tried any drugs, including alcohol or tobacco, and—before we get too hysterical—47 per cent of Canadian high school students "strongly disapprove of regular marijuana smoking."

A Cultural Mainstay

Nevertheless, cannabis remains the No. 1 illicit drug in North America. And its reputation may be shifting, as science uncovers new medical potential for the cannabinoids that are the active ingredients in marijuana. Last month, a Saskatchewan study reported that a cannabis-like substance injected into rats caused new nerve-cell growth in the hippocampus, suggesting the possibility that marijuana might actually improve certain brain functions—contrary to its reputation as a memory-shredder. (It should be added that the rats were getting a drug 100 times more powerful than THC, the compound that gives marijuana its high.) A study published in a recent issue of the journal *Nature* also suggested that marijuana may "more closely resemble an antidepressant than a drug of abuse." And, of course, the much-debated medical benefits of cannabis for people suffering with chronic pain, AIDS or multiple sclerosis are already well known.

Marijuana is also firmly embedded in popular culture, from the slim green leaves featured on the cover of Willie Nelson's recent CD (reggae, of course), to the phenomenon of "bud porn" (coffee-table books featuring photos of dewy, resin-oozing exotic strains of cannabis), to *Weeds*, the new series currently airing on Showcase. It stars Mary-Louise Parker as a freshly widowed mother who supports her family by dealing pot in her upscale Californian suburb. ("But not to kids," she explains, setting the moral high bar of the show.)

The series traffics in lame stereotypes (her suppliers are a trash-talkin' black family whose mother cleans and bags her product at the kitchen table). But it flies in the face of George W. Bush's $35-billion War on Drugs, which focuses many of its public awareness programs on the evils of smoking pot while largely ignoring the scourge of crystal meth use in North America. And it's one more sign that marijuana is not about to be weeded out of the culture any time soon.

If this is the case, what sort of limits should parents offer, when their 13-year-old comes home from a party to announce—because they encourage the kid to be open—that he has just smoked his first joint? Of course, they turn off David Letterman, pour a glass of wine, sit down and say, "We don't want you smoking marijuana, sweetheart. You're too young." Then he says, with a red-eyed glare, "Why not? You do."

How does a parent respond to that? With a lecture on how dope impairs concentration and learning, and may not be the best thing for the lungs? Or with a mini-joint and some Neil Young on the CD player?

The Pot (Smoker) Calling the Kettle Black

"When it comes to my own son, I'm totally protective—I veer right into *Reefer Madness* [a 1936 propaganda film on the dangers of marijuana] territory," says Ray, a Toronto father and regular grass smoker who was introduced to hash at the age of 15 by his own, scientist father. (Note: not even the most nonchalant pot smoker would agree to be named here. Apparently no one, 15 or 55, wants to be known as a pot-head—or arrested. So the names and some identifying details in these stories have been changed.)

"When my son asked if I smoked dope, I simply lied and said no," Ray continues. "But his older sister was with us. She knew that I smoked, and said, 'What are you talking about, dad? Of course you do!'" But Ray's double standard is just fine with his son; kids don't necessarily want their parents to be cool. The writer and film director Nora Ephron once observed that if children are given the choice between a happy, gratified parent off boogie-boarding in Hawaii, or a suicidal parent in the next room, they'll pick the miserable, available one every time. The baby boomer pursuit of pleasure and openness may have produced parents who resemble party-hearty older siblings rather than helpful, boring authority figures. "Even though in the real world, marijuana may occupy an unclear, grey zone," says Bob Glossop, a spokesman for the Vanier Institute for the Family, "one of the roles of the parent is to simplify their kids' world, and offer limits."

Some parents are open about their dope smoking while drawing firm lines about drug use for their kids. Patrick is a Toronto writer, poet, parent and cannabis fan. He finds a joint in the late afternoon helps him write. "When my son confronted me and said, 'But you do it,' I said, 'Yes, I smoke pot, but I also earn a living. You are 12 and in Grade 8 and you shouldn't smoke marijuana." Patrick mostly confines his habit to his workspace, but he has always smoked in the house. "My line with my two sons was clear. I told them, 'If you want to finish your education, don't smoke weed.' It tends to demotivate kids regarding school. I know it brought out my own rebellion, and made me want to quit school and fight the system."

Patrick's relationship to marijuana goes back 27 years, when his stepson, then six, entered his life. "The vibe around pot smoking was different then; it was a more legitimate activity. I smoked in the house, but I explained to my stepson that it was an herb—coltsfoot—that I had to smoke, for my lungs." He sounds a bit sheepish here. "So, yeah, it was a lie, but not entirely; it was an herbal supplement."

His stepson grew up to become a very conservative adult, and a non-smoker, but "surprisingly tolerant" of marijuana. "Coltsfoot has become a kind of joke between us," says Patrick.

When he had his own sons, they both ignored his advice and took up dope smoking around 13. His eldest, Richard, then started dealing; he encountered some violence, got robbed, and finally decided that the dope life was not a good one. "Although I do think he honed his business skills when he was selling," Patrick muses. "He was making good money." Gradually, Richard gave up dope. "He saw that all his friends were dropping out of school, and he didn't want to. He's now in university, studying philosophy, doing well, and he rarely smokes pot. He'd rather argue about philosophy now, which drives me crazy, because . . ."—and here the truly committed pot smoker can be detected—"it's so damn rational."

But Patrick remembers his sons' drug years as a "worrying time. I was really concerned." And he's not alone. Parents worry about the dangers associated with the criminal aspect of marijuana—which is, after all, still an illegal substance, carrying a maximum fine of $1,000 and/or six months in jail for simple possession. The government may be pondering the wisdom of spending millions on imprisoning cannabis offenders when gunshot deaths seem to be everywhere, and white collar crime flies under the radar. With 69 per cent of Canadians favouring decriminalization of pot possession, according to a February 2003 poll, the feds have taken a step to acknowledging the country's dope use. Last year, they introduced a bill that would decriminalize possession of small amounts of cannabis. But it's currently sitting with a Commons committee and is unlikely to become law before the next federal election.

As they step out onto their back decks to have a quick after-dinner toke, noticing that thick feeling in their lungs again, parents also worry about the long-term effects of marijuana on a 13-year-old's developing mind and body. (Many experts believe regular pot smoking damages the lungs, though there's debate over whether it's more or less harmful than tobacco.) And then there's the school issue: chronic use is linked to declining school work and dropping out.

One Toke Too Many over the Line

Young people who have already smoked marijuana for a decade are discovering what some of their parents know—it is more habit-forming than its reputation suggests. Eric, who works as a fly-fishing guide near Vancouver, is 19 and has been smoking pot daily—except for the brief periods when he's tried to stop—for about seven years. He lives in a province where more than half the population has tried pot and many are regular users.

Eric's parents were both involved in the political upheaval of the sixties. His mother once spent a night in jail for possession of pot, and, Eric says, "my father told me that he tried everything once, which I tend to believe." Eric's dad, Dmitri, is now a criminal psychologist who is in favour of the legalization of marijuana—although he no longer smokes it himself, and dearly wishes his son would stop too. Despite his liberal perspective, Dmitri views the heavy pot smoking among his son's circle as "insidiously costly." Eric—whom his father proudly describes as a "beautiful, athletic, creative, sensitive young man"—couldn't agree more.

"I would like to quit, a lot," Eric says. "And every single friend I know who smokes heavily wants to stop too. Dope is okay in moderation, but when your life starts to revolve around it every day, it becomes like any other addiction. You lose your motivation. Your senses get numbed. And you don't get out of life what you could if you weren't stoned all the time. It was fun to party at 14. But the older you get, the more you kind of want to pull up your socks and get your life going. I've quit a few times, but it's hard. I don't even have to go out and buy it—it's all around me."

Bestselling American health and wellness author Dr. Andrew Weil could not be called anti-pot by any stretch. And the 2004 edition of his book, *From Chocolate to Morphine*, is an unhysterical guide to a wide spectrum of mind-altering drugs. But Weil is very clear about the risks of habitual use. "Marijuana dependence can be sneaky in its development," he writes. "It doesn't appear overnight like cigarette addiction . . . but rather builds up over a long time. The main danger of smoking marijuana is simply that it will get away from you, becoming more and more of a repetitive habit and less and less of a useful way of changing consciousness."

Elizabeth Ridgely is a Toronto therapist and executive director of the George Hull Centre for Children and Families, which has a substance-abuse program open to heavy pot smokers. "The most important thing for parents to know is that marijuana is stronger than it used to be in the Woodstock days," she says. "People who use it habitually use it to soothe themselves, and when they stop, they can feel agitated and anxious. It can really mess up a kid. But kids are surprised to hear this—families aren't having those kinds of conversations about drugs."

Dreams Gone Up in Smoke

"We call them Jell-O-heads," says Tanya, a 52-year-old photo-archivist who lives in Toronto. "Boys who can't really think."

She is referring to her 19-year-old son and his friends, who regularly smoke dope on the third floor of her house. "When they come in the door and go up the stairs, it's like having large cedar trees in the house. Everything shakes and rattles. Then they go up to my son's room, and the music starts, and the laughing."

Tanya is a former pot smoker who now considers dope a "real time-waster." I wasted so many years as a hippie, smoking. But it was part of the language back then. It was social, it was anti-authority, it was very sensual. I don't see that with my son's crowd. They just seem sedated. They use a bong, and the drug is really clean and refined and incredibly potent—it's not the ditch weed we used to smoke. It doesn't give you the big fuzzy body stone we used to get from dope. They just get high. I think it dumbs my kid down. The thing that bothers me is that he doesn't seem present when he's stoned.

"My son gave me some of his dope once," says Tanya. "I thought it would be a good way to, you know, talk about it. I didn't want to smoke, so I ate it, and suddenly my eyelids had no function—I mean, I would close my eyes and it would just go on forever. When will this be over, I thought." After some ineffective drug counselling, her son eventually cut down on his own. "Now he says he only smokes it to get to sleep, as a sedative." She laughs. "Remember when we thought smoking marijuana made us more aware?"

A friend of Tanya's, a Gestalt therapist, has a theory about the downside of heavy pot smoking for teenagers. She considers it a "dream-stealer. At the age when they should be generating their own fantasies and dreams, a drug can usurp that. The visions belong to the drug, not to them."

Smokescreen for Other Problems

Mario, a handsome, athletic 23-year-old, went the whole nine yards with drugs and teen rebellion. He started smoking dope, taking acid and staying out till 4 a.m. when he was 12 and 13.

He and his friends would get stoned and go chase skunks through the park in the middle of the night, until somebody called the cops. "If there was a rule, he would break it," remembers his father. He had separated from the boy's mother and was living with his new partner. The separation was civil, and Mario and his younger brother, Paul, were welcome in both households.

"My mother didn't hide the fact that she would smoke around the house occasionally," Mario says. "But she didn't glamorize it. If you're going to have a parent who smokes pot, she went about it the right way. Kids are supersensitive to anything that's hypocritical, especially in their parents. It breaks trust." But his parents worried about the effect Mario's behaviour was having on Paul. They asked him to honour one final rule—no smoking pot in the house, or around his younger brother. When Mario broke that one, his father asked him to move out.

So at the age of 15, for almost two years, Mario was out on the street, couch-surfing at friends' houses and living for a time in a hostel for street kids. He quit school after three weeks of Grade 9. "We gave him money to buy toiletries, which he probably spent on dope," his father says. They stayed in touch, though, and finally his mother said, "That's enough," and let him move in with her. He went back to high school and graduated. He reconnected with the rest of his family, was accepted at Queen's and got a degree in anthropology, and by his late teens had lost interest in pot.

Mario now looks back on those years with hard-earned intelligence and insight. "As far as our family problems go, I think dope was more of a flashpoint than the real issue. My pot smoking was an abrasive thing, and my parents concentrated on that. And it did have tangible fallout—in terms of punctuality and procrastination and school. You know, if a kid isn't getting his work done, and he's smoking dope, it's an easy equation to make. But there's usually more than dope going on."

Poor parents—they always seem to miss the point. And what has become the ultimate parental sin now that pot is out of the closet? Smoking cigarettes. Mario also has a sister, Lucy. At the age of 11, she came home one night to find a dinner party in progress, and her non-smoking mother sitting back with a lit cigarette in hand. "She went ballistic," recalls the mother, "and after everyone left, Lucy came down and sprayed the room with perfume. It was a big deal—kids hate it when their parents do anything self-destructive."

So, a memo to all you law-breaking, pot smoking parents: if you want your kids not to worry, just say no—to tobacco.

Organizations to Contact

The editors have compiled the following list of organizations concerned with the issues presented in this book. The descriptions are derived from materials provided by the organizations. All have publications or information available for interested readers. The list was compiled on the date of publication of the present volume; the information provided here may change. Be aware that many organizations take several weeks or longer to respond to inquiries, so allow as much time as possible.

Cannabis Consumers Campaign (CCC)
PO Box 1716, El Cerrito, CA   94530
(510) 215-8326
e-mail: mikki@cannabisconsumers.org
Web site: www.cannabisconsumers.org

The Cannabis Consumers Campaign (CCC) advocates changing public policy to dispel the myths and negative stereotypes that perpetuate marijuana prohibition and all its harsh consequences. The organization strives to provide a more positive and accurate image of adults who consume cannabis by demonstrating to the general public, the media, and political leaders that pot smokers are good, responsible, contributing members of society who deserve equal status and treatment before the law and in society as a whole. The group's Web site includes articles entitled "Equal Rights for Everybody," "The Experience of Getting High," "Debating Marijuana Policy," and "Talk to Your Kids About Pot."

Common Sense for Drug Policy
1377-C Spencer Avenue, Lancaster, PA   17603
(717) 299-0600 • fax: (717) 393-4953
e-mail: info@csdp.org
Web site: www.csdp.org

Common Sense for Drug Policy is a nonprofit organization committed to educating the public about alternatives to current drug policy by disseminating research, hosting public forums, and informing the media. It also gives advice and technical assistance to allied organizations working to reform current drug policy. On its Web site, Common Sense provides access to news articles, data, and research concerning marijuana and other drugs. It also publishes the book *Drug War Facts*, which includes a discussion of marijuana policy.

Drug Enforcement Administration (DEA)

Mailstop: AES, 2401 Jefferson Davis Highway
Alexandria, VA   22301
(202) 307-1000
Web site: www.usdoj.gov/dea

An agency of the U.S. Department of Justice, the Drug Enforcement Administration (DEA) enforces the controlled substances laws and regulations of the United States and brings to justice those involved in the cultivation, manufacture, or distribution of controlled substances appearing in or destined for illicit traffic. In addition, the DEA recommends and supports non-enforcement programs aimed at reducing the availability of illicit controlled substances on the domestic and international markets. Its publications include *Drugs of Abuse*, which features a chapter on Marijuana; *Get It Straight: The Facts About Drugs*, and *Speaking Out Against Drug Legalization*.

Drug Policy Alliance (DPA)

70 West Thirty-sixth Street, Sixteenth Floor
New York, NY   10018
(212) 613-8020 • fax: (212) 613-8021
e-mail: nyc@drugpolicy.org
Web site: www.drugpolicy.org

The Drug Policy Alliance (DPA) is an organization dedicated to ending the U.S. federal government's war on drugs. Instead, the DPA advocates implementing progressive drug policies based on science, compassion, health, and human rights. Chief among the organization's stated goals is to make marijuana legally available for medical use and to end criminal penalties for marijuana, except those involving distribution of drugs to children. Publications include *Marijuana: The Facts, What's Wrong with the Drug War?* and *Safety First: Parents, Teens, and Drugs.*

DrugSense
14252 Culver Drive #328, Irvine, CA   92604-0326
(800) 266-5759
e-mail info@drugsense.org
Web site: www.drugsense.org

DrugSense is committed to raising public awareness about the damage caused by the war on drugs in the United States, informing the public about rational alternatives to the drug war, and helping organize citizens to bring about drug policy reforms. The organization promotes public debate and discussion of current drug policy and provides online and technical support to allied reform groups. Through its Media Awareness Project, DrugSense maintains a database called the Drugnews Archive, which contains current news and opinion articles about drugs and drug policy, including marijuana. The organization also publishes the newsletter *DrugSense Weekly.*

Marijuana Policy Project (MPP)
PO Box 77492, Capitol Hill, Washington, DC   20013
(202) 462-5747
e-mail: info@mpp.org
Web site:www.mpp.org

The Marijuana Policy Project (MPP) is dedicated to forming public policy that allows for the responsible medical and non-medical use of marijuana and minimizes the problems associated with marijuana consumption and the laws that manage its use. The organization's stated mission is to make marijuana medically available to patients in need and to tax and regulate marijuana for general adult use. The MPP strives to reach these goals by increasing public support for marijuana regulation; identifying and activating supporters of medical marijuana and marijuana regulation; changing state laws to legalize medical marijuana and/or regulate marijuana; and increasing the credibility of marijuana policy reform. Publications include the *Marijuana Policy Report*, a quarterly newsletter.

National Center on Addiction and Substance Abuse (CASA) at Columbia University

633 Third Avenue, Nineteenth Floor
New York, NY 10017-6706
(212) 841-5200 • fax: (212) 956-8020
Web site: www.casacolumbia.org

The National Center on Addiction and Substance Abuse (CASA) at Columbia University is a nonprofit organization whose goal is to inform Americans about the economic and social costs of substance abuse and its impact on their lives. CASA employs an interdisciplinary staff of more than sixty professionals with post-graduate and doctorate degrees, who have experience and expertise in various fields, including substance abuse and addiction, communications, criminology, education, epidemiology, government, law, journalism, psychology, public administration, health and policy, social work, sociology, and statistics. In addition to a quarterly newsletter, CASA's publications include the articles "Non-Medical Marijuana II: Rite of Passage or Russian Roulette?" "Teen Cigarette Smoking and Marijuana Use," and "National Survey of American Attitudes on Substance Abuse XI: Teens and Parents."

National Clearinghouse for Alcohol and Drug Information (NCADI)

PO Box 2345, Rockville, MD 20847-2345
(800) 729-6686 • fax: (240) 221-4292
e-mail: ncadi-info@samhsa.hhs.gov
Web site:www.ncadi.samhsa.gov

Managed by the Substance Abuse and Mental Health Services Administration (SAMHSA), the National Clearinghouse for Alcohol and Drug Information (NCADI) provides the most up-to-date and comprehensive information about substance abuse prevention and treatment in the United States. NCADI offers more than five hundred items to the public from various government agencies that produce materials related to substance abuse. The clearinghouse also employs information specialists who can recommend appropriate publications, posters, and videocassettes; conduct customized searches; provide grant and funding information; and refer people to appropriate organizations. Publications include *Marijuana: Facts Parents Need to Know*, *Marijuana: Facts for Teens*, and *Tips for Teens: The Truth About Marijuana*.

National Institute on Drug Abuse (NIDA)
6001 Executive Boulevard, Room 5213
Bethesda, MD   20892-9561
(301) 443-1124
e-mail: information@nida.nih.org
Web site: www.nida.nih.org

A research agency of the U.S. government and the part of the National Institutes of Health, National Institute on Drug Abuse (NIDA) conducts scientific studies concerning the causes and effects of drug abuse. The organization distributes the results of its research to policy makers, practitioners, and the general public. NIDA's many publications include *Marijuana: Facts for Teens*, *NIDA Infofacts: Marijuana*, *Marijuana: Facts Parents Need to Know*, and *NIDA Research Report Series: Marijuana*.

National Organization for the Reform of Marijuana Laws (NORML)
1600 K Street NW, Suite 501, Washington, DC   20006-2832
(202) 483-5500 • fax: (202) 483-0057
e-mail: norml@norml.org
Web site: www.norml.org

Since its founding in 1970, the National Organization for the Reform of Marijuana Laws (NORML) has been the principal advocate for ending the prohibition of marijuana in the United States. The organization lobbies state and federal legislators to permit the medical use of marijuana and to decriminalize marijuana for personal use. It publishes two quarterly reports, the *NORML Legislative Bulletin* and the *NORML Leaflet*. On its Web site, NORML provides access to its weekly news bulletin, as well as studies and testimony concerning marijuana.

Office of National Drug Control Policy (ONDCP)

PO Box 6000, Rockville, MD   20849-6000
(800) 666-3332 • fax: (301) 519-5212
Web site: www.whitehousedrugpolicy.gov

The White House Office of National Drug Control Policy (ONDCP), a component of the Executive Office of the President, is committed to establishing policies, priorities, and objectives to combat the drug control program in the United States. The goals of the ONDCP are to reduce illicit drug use, manufacturing, trafficking, drug-related crime and violence, and drug-related health consequences. To achieve these goals, the director of ONDCP is charged with producing the National Drug Control Strategy. The strategy directs the nation's antidrug efforts and establishes a program, a budget, and guidelines for cooperation among federal, state, and local entities. Publications include *Marijuana Myths & Facts: The Truth Behind 10 Popular Misperceptions, What Americans Need to Know About Marijuana,* and *Who's Really in Jail for Marijuana?*

Parents. The Anti-Drug.

PO Box 6000, Rockville, MD   20849-6000
(800) 666-3332 • fax: (301) 519-5212
Web site: www.theantidrug.com

TheAntiDrug.com was created by the National Youth Anti-Drug Media Campaign to equip parents and other adult caregivers with the tools they need to raise drug-free children. The organization collaborates with leading U.S. experts in the fields of parenting and substance-abuse prevention. In addition, the group serves as a drug prevention information center, as well as a support network where parents can interact and learn from each other. Publications include *TheAntiDrug.*

com Parenting Tips Newsletter, Marijuana Resources for Parents and Key Influencers, and *Keeping Your Kids Drug-Free: A How-to Guide for Parents and Caregivers.*

Partnership for a Drug-Free America

405 Lexington Avenue, Suite 1601, New York, NY   10174
(212) 922-1560 • fax: (212) 922-1570
Web site: www.drugfreeamerica.org

A coalition of professionals from the communications industry, the Partnership for a Drug-Free America is dedicated to reducing the demand for illegal drugs via media communication. Through its national antidrug advertising campaign, the organization strives to change societal attitudes of support or toleration toward drug use. In addition, it conducts annual studies on the current attitudes of Americans toward drug use and abuse, which are available on its Web site. The organization publishes the monthly *Partnership Bulletin* and the biannual *Newsletter of the Partnership for a Drug-Free America.*

Stop the Drug War

1623 Connecticut Avenue NW, Third Floor
Washington, DC   20009
(202) 293-8340 • fax: (202) 293-8344
e-mail drcnet@drcnet.org
Web site: www.stopthedrugwar.org

Stop the Drug War is an advocacy group created by the Drug Reform Coordination Network (DRCNet), an organization committed to ending drug prohibition worldwide and replacing it with a sensible regime of control through regulation. In the interim, DRCNet supports philosophically compatible policy reforms and programs to reduce the excesses of the drug war and its attendant harms. DRCNet works for these objectives through educational programs, lobbying efforts focusing on U.S. lawmakers, and through providing support to allied reform groups. DRCNet's principal publication is the online weekly drug policy newsletter, *The Drug War Chronicle.*

Bibliography

Books

Martin Booth	*Cannabis: A History.* New York: St. Martin's, 2003.
Timmen L. Cermak	*Marijuana: What's a Parent to Believe?* Center City, MN: Hazelden, 2003.
Mitch Earleywine, ed.	*Pot Politics: Marijuana and the Costs of Prohibition.* Oxford, UK: Oxford University Press, 2007.
Mitch Earleywine, ed.	*Understanding Marijuana: A New Look at the Scientific Evidence.* Oxford, UK: Oxford University Press, 2002.
James P. Gray	*Why Our Drug Laws Have Failed and What We Can Do About It: A Judicial Indictment of the War on Drugs.* Philadelphia: Temple University Press, 2001.
Ansley Hamid	*The Ganja Complex: Rastafari and Marijuana.* Lanham, MD: Lexington, 2002.
Douglas N. Husak	*Legalize This! The Case for Decriminalizing Drugs.* London: Verso, 2002.
Margaret O. Hyde and John F. Setaro	*Drugs 101: An Overview for Teens.* Brookfield, CT: Twenty-First Century, 2003.

Thomas A. Jacobs — *They Broke the Law—You Be the Judge: True Cases of Teen Crime.* Minneapolis, MN: Free Spirit, 2003.

Dean Kuipers — *Burning Rainbow Farm: How a Stoner Utopia Went Up in Smoke.* New York: Bloomsbury, 2006.

Robert J. MacCoun and Peter Reuter — *Drug War Heresies: Learning from Other Vices, Times, and Places.* Cambridge, UK: Cambridge University Press, 2001.

Jeffrey A. Miron — *The Budgetary Implications of Marijuana Prohibition.* Washington, DC: Marijuana Policy Project, June 2005.

Office of National Drug Control Policy — *Marijuana Myths and Facts: The Truth Behind 10 Popular Misperceptions.* Office of National Drug Control Policy, November 2004.

Brian Preston — *Pot Planet: Adventures in Global Marijuana Culture.* New York: Grove, 2002.

Pauline Reilly — *Cannabis & Cancer: Arthur's Story.* Melbourne: Scribe Publications, 2001.

Eric Schlosser — *Reefer Madness: Sex, Drugs, and Cheap Labor in the American Black Market.* Boston: Houghton Mifflin, 2003.

Periodicals

Joseph V. Amodio — "Why Pot's Not Cool," *Current Health*, March 11–12, 2005.

Paul Armentano   "You Are Going Directly to Jail. DUID Legislation: What It Means, Who's Behind It, and Strategies to Prevent It," National Organization for the Reform of Marijuana Laws, August 26, 2006.

Doug Bandow   "Which Side is Winning the War on Drugs?" *San Diego Union-Tribune,* May 13, 2004.

B. Bower   "Marijuana's Risks Become Blurrier," *Science News,* May 22, 2004.

Judith S. Brook, David W. Brook, Orlando Arencibia-Mireles, Linda Richter, and Martin Whiteman   "Risk Factors for Adolescent Marijuana Use Across Cultures and Across Time," *Journal of Genetic Psychology,* September 2001.

William F. Buckley, Jr.   "Reefer Madness," *National Review,* July 14, 2003.

Jonathan P. Caulkins and Eric L. Sevigny   "How Many People Does the U.S. Imprison for Drug Use, and Who Are They?" *Contemporary Drug Problems,* Fall 2005.

Alexander Cockburn   "The Right Not to Be in Pain," *Nation,* February 3, 2003.

DRCNet   "DRCNet Interview: Marijuana Policy Project Director Rob Kampia," *Drug War Chronicle,* February 11, 2005.

Robert Dreyfuss　　"Bush's War on Pot," *Rolling Stone*, July 28, 2005.

Mitch Earleywine　"The Potent Pot Myth," *DrugSense* and Bruce Mirken　*Weekly*, July 23, 2004.

Dan Gardner　　　"Is Pot More Potent than in the Past?" *Ottawa Citizen* (Canada), March 19, 2005.

Andrew D.　　　　"Cannabis Careers Reconsidered: Hathaway　　　　　Transitions and Trajectories of Committed Long-Term Users," *Contemporary Drug Problems*, Fall 2004.

Dan Hurley　　　　"Medicinal Marijuana on Trial," *New York Times*, March 29, 2005.

Sid Kirchheimer　　"Heavy Marijuana Use Doesn't Damage Brain," *WebMD Medical News*, July 1, 2003.

Kenneth E.　　　　"Changes in Marijuana Use Over the Leonard and　　　Transition into Marriage," *Journal of* Gregory G.　　　　*Drug Issues*, Spring 2005. Homish

Damon Linker　　　"Going to Pot?" *First Things*, November 2001.

Richard Lowry　　　"Weed Whackers," *National Review*, August 20, 2001.

Robert MacCoun　　"Marijuana, Heroin, and Cocaine," and Peter Reuter　　*American Prospect*, June 3, 2002.

David　　　　　　　"High Society," *Independent on Sunday* McCandless　　　　(UK), September 4, 2005.

Neo K. Morojele and Judith S. Brook — "Adolescent Precursors of Intensity of Marijuana and Other Illicit Drug Use Among Adult Initiators," *Journal of Genetic Psychology*, December 2001.

Brian L. Muldrew — "Drug Enforcement: Controlled Substances Act Inapplicable to Medical Marijuana," *Journal of Law, Medicine, and Ethics*, Summer 2004.

Ethan A. Nadelmann — "The Future of an Illusion," *National Review*, September 27, 2004.

National Survey on Drug Use and Health — "How and Where Young Adults Obtain Marijuana," in the *NSDUH Report*, Office of Applied Studies, Substance Abuse and Mental Health Services Administration (SAMHSA), 2006.

National Youth Anti-Drug Media Campaign — "Marijuana and Teens: Fact Sheet," National Youth Anti-Drug Media Campaign, August 2, 2004.

Evelyn Nieves — "Half an Ounce of Healing," *Mother Jones*, January–February 2001.

Pamela Paul — "Marijuana Attitude Shift," *American Demographics*, June 2003.

Joseph M. Rey, Andrés Martin, and Peter Krabman — "Is the Party Over? Cannabis and Juvenile Psychiatric Disorder: The Past 10 Years," *Journal of the American Academy of Child and Adolescent Psychiatry*, October 2004.

Nina Riccio — "What You Should Know About Marijuana," *Current Health*, January 2003.

Peter Schrag	"A Quagmire for Our Time," *American Prospect*, August 13, 2001.
John P. Walters	"No Surrender," *National Review*, September 27, 2004.
Montel Williams	"Fighting for Your Life Shouldn't Be a Crime," *Chicago Tribune*, February 14, 2005.
Tim Wu	"The WTO: The Stoner's New Best Friend," *Slate*, March 17, 2005.

Index